NONCHALANT PERFECTIONISM

Man's Guide to Developing Emotional Resilience

ETHAN R. GIBSON

Table of Contents

For my Mother and Father

Preface

Let me be honest, I didn't think people read the preface to any book. I, for one, have never read a preface all the way through. My thought process was simple, "what I *need* to know will be written in the book, which I'm already about to read. No need for the preface." which was followed by the inquisitive question of, "why do they even write these?" Soon, that question was followed by not reading the entire book. Needless to say, I wasn't a strong fan of prefaces, or books, or reading.

Well, 20-year-old me would be very surprised to learn that the older, and obviously much wiser, 24-year-old version of himself now is writing the very thing he never read. Even more shocking to him would be the amount of times I had to read and reread this one preface! Well despite my unwillingness to read a preface, I am now much more appreciative of them. Towards the end of the book, I realized there were a few overarching points I'd like to state before you dive into it. A few things need to be said to let you know what you're getting yourself into. So, I figured a preface would be perfect. As a matter of fact, when I first had the idea for the preface, I said "why don't more people write prefaces?" Irony sure has a way of making fun of us, doesn't it?

I will begin with this: I am neither a clinical psychologist nor a clinical psychiatrist. I do not have the necessary education to accurately diagnose your mental health issues. I cannot write you prescriptions or determine which combination of drugs would supplement your mental health. Now, while I could probably find a way to get pills illegally, I'm told that's both immoral and unethical. So, we're out of luck there.

Furthermore, I don't suggest that the principles discussed in these pages are the answer to those whose mental illnesses are at such a level where they cannot function on their own. There are those of us out there who have got the short end of the stick and live in a permanent state of constant need for supervision. My heart goes out to them, and I do hope that just maybe something from my experiences could be applicable to them. Though I'm sure their complex challenges require solutions I am incapable of offering.

What I've written, I think, will have the highest chance to help the vast majority of us. Those of us who are average. Those of us who believe our impact on the world will be little. Those of us who patiently keep trying to improve. Much like the Mormon Pioneers of the mid 1800s, we solemnly pick up our handcarts, continuing our journey despite its duration and disappointments. We live at the center of this human condition. The human condition, as life has been called, is a shared experience among every one of us. You can't escape this condition. Birth immediately inducted you into this human issue. We're all here, now. Some have figured ways to excel, amassing wealth, fame and power; they are deemed to be living in prosperity. Others have very little in terms of material wealth, status, and acclaim; they are deemed to be living in poverty. Between these far distant lifestyles lies people who occasionally fluctuate between the two, yet ultimately remain in the middle; they are living in the populous. And so, your human condition can only *look* different from others. Yet, as the common denominator among all human's condition, it all *feels* very similar. Based on personal experiences, I have derived principles intended to help you, and me, throughout these long lived days.

I had to start with my lack of formal education in this area because if you are reading in hopes to learn from a PhD in this field, you will undoubtedly be disappointed. Matter of fact, I dropped out of college—twice.

Now, if you're still reading, it is much appreciated! Though I do not have a formal education, I do think of myself qualified to talk on these subjects, however. Just, not from a *clinical* standpoint. A degree of any level was not required to learn ways through my clinical depression. A degree, then, is not required to share my experience.

Deriving from my personal life, the book is more or less anecdotal. Anecdotal solutions to anecdotal problems. My purpose is not to deliver groundbreaking research that I found while running experiments. No, my purpose is much more informal. Much more personal. I would like to share with you what has helped keep me above water. On that note, this book is not intended to replace therapy or become one's main source of guidance through life's traumatizing curriculum. The purpose lies solely in helping you help yourself through simple expressions of rather complicated experiences. If anything in this book helps you, that's fantastic. If nothing in this book helps you, that's also fantastic. Because you then get the opportunity to develop your own methods, principles, and personal solutions. If I knew your personal experiences, then maybe I could be more helpful. Unfortunately, I know almost nothing about you.

Knowing no personal experiences about you and not much about those personal experiences of close family, I am left to dissect my own in order to convey my message. As such, I want it absolutely clear that none of what I share regarding my achievements come from a place of self-righteousness, contempt, conceit, or self-aggrandizement. I do not care about being seen by you in a certain light, and have not written this book in a meticulous way to create a light to be seen in. What I share comes from a place of authenticity, and, at the very least, that's all I can be. Welcome to *Nonchalant Perfectionism,* and thank you for reading the preface.

"Pretty sure I'll think of a good quote to put here. Yeah, I'll think of something."

- Ethan Ross Gibson

SECTION 1

Chapter 1
Invigorating Backwash

Sunday morning, October 21st, 2018, in Pensacola, Florida, I was a missionary serving a small Spanish community in Florida. My missionary companion and I were asked to give a sermon that morning. We sat on the rostrum, waiting for our 15 minutes to speak on the Gospel of Jesus Christ. The congregation was sizable but not the largest I've spoken to. Even before being a missionary, I effortlessly spoke to a crowd of at least 300 people. Familiar with public speaking, this was nothing worth fretting over. Prepared and ready to go, I felt mildly nervous, as was common. That morning, I had gone through my typical routine when assigned to speak: a light breakfast, plenty of water, and reviewing my notes to the point of memorization. Committing the words to memory allows me to follow along with the script in my head while looking/engaging with the audience. Then, I can throw in a few adlibs (mostly jokes) if I feel so inclined (which I always feel so inclined) and fall back into place. My missionary companion was very well prepared, and I thoroughly enjoyed his talk. After he spoke, there was a youth speaker. Talking faster than he could think, he lasted a tight five minutes. Rather impressive, in my opinion. I'm pretty sure his seat was still warm when he sat down.

At this point, the entire congregation arose to sing a hymnal. Watching 300 people stand up at once always surprises me. Always loud and disruptive, it snapped me out of my pensive thoughts. Have you ever stood up too quickly, and your vision goes blurry for a second? Then you start seeing what looks like the edge of the galaxy, and it feels like you're really there because you're probably light-headed too. Once I stood up, I was deep in that galaxy. Keeping my composure, I pretended to sing along to the hymn. After all, I stood in front of and in clear view of hundreds of people. I feared just one of them would see me dazed, and Heaven forbid they see any weakness shine through. I've got an image to keep, and looking light-headed or pale-faced was far from that image. The hymn progressed, and suddenly, the organ sounded muffled, as if someone put foam in each of its pipes. Everyone singing now sounded like they were only humming. Panicking, I rubbed my eyes to clear my blurred vision, only to be hit with nausea like I'd never felt before. In a matter of seconds, my highly scrutinized image burned to bits because suddenly, I could not hear, see, or think clearly. I only remember fearing not being able to appropriately deliver my prepared message. My well-being was not my priority; rather, it was my image. Turning to my companion, I said, "Yo, I don't feel so good... I jus-" My nervous system was unprepared for that sudden movement and immediately shut down. Vision going black and taking strength from my legs; I somehow awoke sitting in my chair, which was followed by an attempt to stand back up and then black unconsciousness. Then I regained consciousness, and with no recollection of how I got there, I laid on my back, staring up at the ceiling, confused as ever.

Immediately after regaining consciousness, my mind was awake and active. Like a river destroying a dam, all my emotions and thoughts poured into my head. Confusion first took center stage, trying to figure out what happened and why all these people were crowding around me, staring at me as if I had leprosy. In a matter of seconds, I pieced together that something must've happened. I must've fallen and hit my head. Otherwise, why would these people be so concerned? In this particular congregation, I knew of two or three medical professionals. At least two of them were in the audience that day, one of whom sat close to me on the rostrum. My eyes would not stay open. They would open briefly for one second and close for ten, twenty, or thirty. I struggled to keep them open longer than a few seconds. In those few moments, and out of my peripheral vision, I recognized the doctor who sat nearest me. Immediately, I knew who he was, his name, and his profession, and I remembered eating with his family a few weeks prior. This only added to my state of confusion. I had no ability to move anything but my eyes, and yet I was aware of the commotion around me. Confusion quickly and forcefully renounced center stage as rage engulfed my head.

Missionaries are seen on the same level as priests. They are good, righteous young men or women who intend to live a righteous, moral life. They abstain from sex, alcohol, any kind of illicit drugs, swearing, vulgar language, and any forms of entertainment that would distract them from their devotion to God. None of them are perfect, of course. Sometimes, they pass out in front of congregations, but their intention to be close to God manifests in their actions, and so they are seen, sometimes, as angels.

Instantly, as rage took over, there was no room for good, missionary behavior. On the outside, I was just a kid that passed out. To hear the thoughts running through my mind would have upset every old lady and mother in that congregation that day. Never before, or since, had I put together a string of words as long, inappropriate, vulgar, or flagrant as I did that day. No one person was safe from the beratement between my ears. I cursed everyone to high Heaven. In a loving manner, they asked, "Can you tell me what year it is?" to which, in my head, I would reply, "Are you ****** kidding me, you son of a *****? For ***** sake, I know what *** **** year it is. You're the *********** idiot you piece of ****, ****!" only to actually answer the only way I physically could, "...it's...twe-nty...twenty..eight...eight-teen?"

"OK, good. Good. Do you know your name? [to another member of the congregation] "Did you call an ambulance? He's been out too long.'

In my head:

"Holy ****! Why the **** do you ****** want to know my ******* name? Can you *********** not see my ******* name tag? (missionaries do wear black name tags with a title. mine read *Elder Gibson*) I mean, c'mon man, this is ****** up. ****

you and all you *********. Goodness ******* gracious, of course, you *****, of course, I know my own ******** name, ok? I'm over this ********. ******* ****! ****!

Actual response:

"Um...ye-yeah...my nam-name i-is...it's...um...Eth-Ethan-Gi-...uh...Gib-Gibson"

The doctors did what they knew best and considered my blood sugar was dangerously low. They asked the congregation if there were any sugary snacks. Fruit snacks, candy, or anything like that. They really needed some sugary drinks, however, because I could not chew. Luckily a lady, and to this day, I don't know who, had some pineapple juice in a sippy cup for their kid.

"Ok, Ethan, we are going to lift your head and tilt it back so you can swallow some of this juice. The sucrose will raise your blood sugar. Then you should start feeling better, alright?"

Actual response:

"Oh...o-ok"

In my head:

"Wow. That's ***** smart. That's just ****** great, isn't it? Congratu-*****-lations. You cracked the **** code. I cannot wait to drink that toddler backwash **** special" [as they gently grabbed, tilted my head] "DON'T ******* TOUCH ME YOU *****! **** this ********** ****. *** ****! ******* HOLY ****! AHHHH I HATE THIS ****, I HATE ALL OF YOU *****!

Apparently, that sucrose must've worked because that was the last intense, rageful outburst I remember. Toddler backwash did the trick! Noticing a shift in attention, I could tell the ambulance had arrived. From those last words I spoke to my companion to when the paramedics lifted me onto the stretcher, I can only imagine about 45 minutes passed by. From what I'm told, for about 20 minutes of that 45, I was unconscious. Out cold. Unresponsive. The ambulance was called after three minutes of unresponsiveness. From getting the toddler backwash special to the ambulance arriving felt like the blink of an eye to me because it literally was. I have no recollection of time passing. From lying on my back on the stage of a church building to laying on a stretcher in an ambulance, it all felt no more than a few seconds. The short dialogue between them and me lasted maybe 30 seconds. I have no recollection of the spaces between questions.

Once at the hospital, the tests began. They ran a slew of tests to determine the cause of my passing out. What actual tests they did, I have no idea. Partly because I don't speak in doctor abbreviations and partly because it wasn't until about a half hour in the hospital that I felt like my normal self. They gave me an IV, had me pee in a plastic urinal, and put all the sticky probes all over my body. Even gave me my own wristbands labeled with my name on a sticker, which they had an entire sheet of. Before I was discharged, I did, in fact, take the entire sheet. I still have it to this day. Gotta love hospital souvenirs!

Luckily, the doctor who first helped me at the church building was the one who helped me at the hospital. He worked there and knew the story from falling to the stretcher. I was probably his easiest patient that day; at least, I hope I was. He entered the room smiling, and so I assumed the worst. I've never really trusted doctors. They seem to always have bad news, maybe because all the time spent with one was under less than pleasant circumstances.

"Elder Gibson," he said (all male missionaries are called *Elder* followed by their last name), "We don't know why you passed out. You're sure you've been drinking enough water?"

I nodded in the affirmative.

"You've been eating?"

I nod, and my missionary companion adds, "He eats breakfast every morning and drinks water. Does that more than I do!"

The doctor resumes, "You are healthy. Your blood sugar was a little low - you're not diabetic?"

"No."

"Well, no results from our test indicate any reason why you should've passed out. We'll release you. Go home and get some rest. You have my phone number, so call if you need anything."

Laying in the hospital bed and hearing that news only enraged me. Though too exhausted to say much, I only put on a smile. What healthy 20-year-old passes out for no reason? Why did this happen? Where was my watch, and why was it not on my wrist? What am I supposed to do now? When will this happen again?

In the dissecting of this and other experiences, I have come to crave stronger emotional resilience. As Charles Swindoll puts it: "Life is ten percent what happens to you and ninety percent how you respond to it." (Swindoll, n.d.). If this statement is true, then we ought to learn how to better respond to that wild, arbitrary "ten percent" that consistently brings us to our knees. Thus, the thesis of this book: to develop emotional resilience.

Chapter 2
What is Emotional Resilience?

Before anyone cares about embarking on self-improvement, for that's what this journey is, there needs to be an underlayment of understanding *what* will be undertaken. For the purposes of this book, emotional resilience will be the facet of self-improvement. Defining emotional resilience creates the attraction in our minds to develop this skill.

- Resilience
- Noun

One: The capability of a strained body to recover its size and shape after deformation caused especially by compressive stress

Two: The ability to recover from or adjust easily to misfortune or change

The above definition completely encompasses my thoughts on what it means to be resilient. In terms of emotion, we are talking about an internal devotion to one's own joy. The crowning characteristic of our internal devotion to a happy life must scream resilience. Without our innermost desire to be resilient, life will trample us under its steel-spiked cleats. Because this topic applies to every human on the planet in a personal way, it becomes incredibly difficult to discuss the interchangeable parts that would result in that personal development. Unfortunately, we are not all the same person (fortunately).

At the time of writing this, the world population recently hit eight billion. Meaning eight billion individual people. Eight billion thoughts almost every second of the day. Eight billion personalities. Eight billion emotional reactions to the day, all day. Eight billion days lived every day. Eight billion sorrows, successes, accomplished dreams, and dashed hopes experienced every day. Eight billion personal experiences every day.

I cannot possibly tell the world what will 100% work for everyone in developing this discipline. No, I don't know all eight billion of you in a way that would conduce your immediate success. Although I wish I was capable of that omniscience, I am only able to put together my few thoughts based on my own experience with the hope it resonates with you. Then, one day, we might meet. And I can stumble through my words to tell you that it will be ok. That you are doing great. You are stronger and better than you think you are. *You are good enough.* Please read that last line once more. If you feel otherwise, determine honestly what you need to change. Then act. I would tell you that I do know for a fact you are capable. Until that day, allow me to list as many of life's punches as I can to *show* what emotional resilience *looks* like. Hopefully, at the very least, I will list just one punch that has hit you. So you can remember that pain in an effort to take the lesson and avoid future pain. I have almost no way to list every hardship in life, but I'm sure you've felt at least one of the following.

- *Romantic relationships end unexpectedly.*
- *Step in dog poop.*
- *Making friends does not come easy.*
- *Boss doesn't know her/his left from their right.*
- *Parents get divorced.*
- *Loose just one AirPod.*
- *Someone close dies. Parent, sibling, child, or close friend.*
- *Flat tire (speaking of an automobile...or the back of your shoe).*
- *Abusive parent(s).*
- *Stub your toe.*
- *Lose the other AirPod.*
- *Rigorous custody battle.*
- *Cat pees all over the kitchen floor or carpeted bedroom.*
- *Abusive lover.*
- *Favorite shirt gets stained.*
- *Hunger.*
- *Start coughing/choking on water.*
- *Laid off from work.*
- *Untied shoelace after already being tied once that day.*
- *Dropped out of college.*
- *Kids eat dirt and don't want to eat their veggies.*

- *Addiction. Personal or that of a close friend or family member.*
- *Suck at video games.*
- *Can't afford expensive video games.*
- *Serious injury from an accident.*
- *Hit your funny bone (not funny).*
- *Favored politician loses.*
- *Favored politician wins.*
- *Admired role model passes away. Or found to be a fraud.*
- *Plans made when feeling social actually have to happen now when not feeling social at all.*
- *Stress in career.*
- *Have to go to work.*
- *Difficulty in deciding life's path.*
- *Can't find any sunglasses.*
- *Friends move away.*
- *Asked to help your friend move (owning a truck)*
- *Friends move onto other people.*
- *Can't find the remote.*
- *Forced to leave a toxic relationship (family member(s), friend(s), partner).*
- *Accidently called boss/teacher/professor your mom or dad.*
- *Hobbies lose their grandeur.*
- *Clog a friend's toilet.*
- *Depression floods every hour of every day.*
- *Clog your toilet.*
- *Anxiety crawls in every fiber of the body.*

- *Clogging any toilet.*
- *Recognition of a loved one moving farther away, emotionally.*
- *Microwave popcorn gets burnt.*
- *Microwave popcorn doesn't burn?*
- *Personal guilt tripping to do more and be more.*
- *Realize at the restaurant you forgot your wallet.*
- *Shame.*
- *Call your date the wrong name (first date).*
- *Deconstruction of faith.*
- *Phone screen cracks.*
- *Detrimental finances, crushing debt.*
- *Forget a name that's been learned before and should be remembered by now.*
- *Watching a close loved one lose their life, personality, and light to drugs.*
- *Have to read a book (possibly this book) for school or work (hopefully not this book).*
- *Tragedy in immediate community, nation, or personal life.*
- *Diarrhea.*
- *Negative beneficiary of poor choices by others.*
- *Fries are forgotten in the drive-thru order.*
- *You get your fries, but they are cold before you get home to thoroughly enjoy them.*

Chances are at least one of the events listed above has plagued your life. No one has an exemption from trauma. In each scenario, the repercussions can damage even the strongest relationships. The affixed emotions are inevitable, and most of us don't know how to properly process our feelings. So, we act out in hundreds of different ways. Our closest friends and family feel our pain of processing. Meaning all hardships in life are indirectly or directly because of another person. More than half of what I listed directly causes pain because of another person. Please remember that very often, these are actions of others, and your trauma response is not intentional on their part. We have no escape from other people, and people have no escape from us. You have an escape from me if you stop reading. I must honor your decision if that is the case. I am grateful you decided to read this far and hope you will continue. Your choice to read or not leads me to the essence of emotional resilience.

All eight billion of us want a life filled with positivity and joy. Emotional resilience strengthens our devotion to that end goal. Emotional resilience bears the burdens of life with an absolute resolve to keep moving forward despite the countless (seemingly) insurmountable obstacles (emotional, physical, or otherwise) presented to you throughout your time in life. Emotional resilience stands at the ready to reset any thwarted course that presents itself as a problem in the aggregation of one's strongest desires. Emotional resilience presently persists onward in the path of self-actualization. Allowing nothing to push it from the very desire pulling it along. Emotional resilience only bends; it does not break, regardless of present pressure. Emotional resilience snaps back into place after being twisted from the solid ground on which it's built. Emotional resilience stubbornly remains constant, consistent, and clear. Emotional resilience creates a deep reverence for life. Emotional resilience appreciates all emotions and doesn't shy away from any, be it positive or negative. Emotional resilience will only lead to benefit oneself. If there ever were a secret to life, I'd argue in favor of emotional resilience 10 out of 10 times.

In an attempt to add validity to my claims of emotional resilience, I am going to cite distinct moments in which I have benefitted from proper processing of my emotions and their resilience. I also will share a few times where the opposite was true, so due to my lack of emotional maturity, I found myself in bigger issues. I will give a general overview of how I grew up and the precise issues I faced. I'd like you to see why I feel so strongly that I have something to offer you. Furthermore, I want to illustrate how growing up in average circumstances still led to trauma. Again, trauma will pass over no one. Rich or poor. Young or old. Luckily, each of us can develop resilience to prosper.

Growing up, until I was 11 years old, I was the youngest of four rambunctious boys and was looked on by them as the runt of the litter. The dynamic surrounding the youngest of four wild animals changed from day to day, yet the oldest consistently sat at the top of the food chain, and I stayed at the bottom. The difference came in which two, or sometimes three, would forget previous grievances and join forces to bully the others. Those few moments when I found favor with my oldest brother were the times I felt validated in who I could be as a man. Together, we'd fight, kick, and bully our other brothers relentlessly. Though enjoyable for me, it would soon end

as the roles would reverse the following day(s). And so went my childhood. Constantly unsure of the love from who I thought would be my closest, dearest friends. Many times, I questioned the support of my parents. I saw my pain at the hands of my brothers as their failure to protect me from harm, which, I thought, was one of their primary roles as my mother and father. This sustained confusion left me relentlessly searching for a way out. Before the age of 11, I had fantasized about suicide, running away from home, and harming my family. I have distinct memories of wanting to kill myself. I have distinct memories of wanting so badly to run away from my family, acting out only a few times. I have distinct memories of wanting to kill my family. Some would say those feelings are expected being the youngest child and would cite frequent temper tantrums from children who have no other way to express themselves. Whether or not I am giving more value to childhood tantrums than deserved, the truth remains in the feelings and memories I vividly remember. Trauma is very personal. Regardless of the medium of trauma, the resulting trauma affects a person the same.

In my case, wanting to abruptly change my circumstances was the root of my trauma. My young, inexperienced response to those circumstances embodied the trauma I grew from. Yes, my brothers did little to help relieve the pain. Yes, my parents may not have been involved every hour of every day (an unrealistic expectation). However, it was my childish coping mechanism that brought me to depression and anxiety.

Wanting to end my life, the life of my loved ones and to abandon my family were all evil thoughts. I recognized they were innately wrong. I knew there was something not right about those thoughts, yet I could not separate the intrusive thoughts from who I was. Thus began my complex with emotions. Growing up in a loving household, I remember constantly being reminded

NONCHALANT PERFECTIONISM   **25**

that my parents loved me. That God loved me. That my extended family loved me. I was, in fact, surrounded by love, so why did I feel so much hate? Not knowing any better, I figured the problem was me. And so was I the solution (a true principle, yet, at the time, executed poorly). To avoid feeling such hatred towards my loved ones, I learned to push all of those emotions deep inside and never let them out. While I didn't feel strong hatred, I became very distant and numb. You can't pick one end of the stick without picking up the other. You can't shove negativity inside without removing positivity. Boxing anger inside, love had no entry. Internalizing no love, there was none to give.

I remember feeling devoid of love beginning around the age of 12. By that age, I had learned how to numb the hatred I felt. I discovered pornography and quickly became dependent on the high it provided. Which only tore apart any sliver of inner joy I had. In this whirlpool of draining emotions, the only thing left was my base-level emotion. A display of any emotion was built from a base of rage. Rage constrained resulted in showing no love to others. All my relationships (familial or otherwise) were surface-level at best. I isolated myself emotionally; I only had a few close friends. My parents and I were not close because I had no idea how to get close to them without feeling rage. And yet, people perceived me as a happy, funny guy. To have others feel attacked due to my lack of love was not an option. While I was incredibly rageful, I made sure others always felt a degree of warmth from me (regardless of its authenticity). Unfortunately, emotions do not dissipate voluntarily. Time does not cure unprocessed, strong emotions; it only marinates them in bitterness. They have to process somehow. I will talk about certain actions that resolve emotions further in the book; for now, I will illustrate how stagnant emotions harrowed away at the innocent joy I once felt.

Growing up with bottled emotions led to violent outbursts in response to seemingly trivial inconveniences. Screaming, wailing, and cursing were the common symptoms with each episode. No one was spared from my rage. Seeing how it hurt others, the decision was made to hurt no one else. Turning to self-hatred, negative self-talk, and pornography, my most volatile emotions had their escape. In an illusion, I thought hurting myself was protecting others. To some degree, it did work. My response to this new cycle of turmoil was a heavy, heavy depression. I do want to add here that I've been diagnosed with clinical depression, and I do understand the reality of such a mental illness. I am not suggesting it was created by my own thoughts and actions. Rather, I gave it the needed fuel it wanted to burn hotter until it consumed me. The further I dove into my depression, the fewer outbursts I had. Therefore, less pain inflicted on my part. In this echo chamber of severe self-deprecation, reassurances of my actions came often. The affixed pain was deep. It hit my heart as it surged through my body like a dull, slow electricity. Like TV static, my head buzzed loudly, and my ears rang. Pornography offered hours of an attractive numbing that became more familiar to me than laughter. I quickly needed more hours viewing it because only then did I feel the dopamine. Knowing full well that when it was over, the numbness would return again. The depression became my soothing balm as the perception of this pain morphed into an idealized comfort. I latched onto depression as a mountain climber would to the secure pitons scattered on the mountain face. The longer I latched, the more soothed I felt. Almost as if depression became the chapstick to my cracked, dry heart. Much like a lip balm, however, always using it results in the constant need for it.

Depression presents an immense danger because the deeper you go into it, the more addictive it becomes. And I was addicted. I built for myself a home in depression. The familiarity of sadness stood alone, comforting me from myself. The absence of love only brings angry hatred. Every day, I centered myself on every menial task. The taskmaster over me punished the concept of self-love and frequently used both anger and depression to fire me up and burn me down. I have to give credit to myself, however, because even though self-criticism ultimately ended in more pain, I was able to accomplish many great things growing up. I found a love for soccer and made it into my high school team. I wrestled in middle school and did well there. Running the 800m in track, I qualified for the city tournament. I excelled in high school, especially in my English classes. Positive things came from constant negativity. It had its advantages, though I don't recommend berating yourself in order to achieve a few goals. That pattern of self-criticism, anger, fear, and depression continued as I graduated high school and went on to the next chapter in my life.

I eventually found the limit of how much self-criticism my mind and body could take. Till all culminated in my brain's involuntary troubleshooting. Allow me to add some context to that story as a means to further illustrate manifestations of childhood coping mechanisms to present struggles.

From the age of 18 to the age of 20, I was a missionary for the Church of Jesus Christ of Latter-Day Saints. Those two formative years were the hardest I had lived and the most rewarding. For those unfamiliar with the responsibilities of a young missionary, I will briefly explain what missionaries do and why those years were extremely difficult. As a missionary, you are assigned an area (anywhere in the world) in which you live and serve the community. More often than not, you are sent far from home. For example, I have friends from Idaho who went to Argentina, some to Africa, a few to Asia, and the Philippines, others to England, and some to Europe. There are many options, afterall we live in a large world. I was blessed to be sent all the way to the deep south of the United States of America, namely Alabama and Florida. Going to a foreign country, you are expected to learn the language of that nation/ mission. Luckily, I was given the opportunity to learn Spanish as it was my assignment to serve the Spanish community in the various cities I lived in. Once settled in, you are tasked with sharing the message of the Gospel, found within the canonical scriptures of the Church of Jesus Christ (Holy Bible and Book of Mormon mainly). For missionaries, they leave everything familiar to them to live in a place they have never been, with a missionary companion they have never met, possibly speaking a language they've never spoken, and their objective to share the Gospel gets overlooked by a vast majority of the people they attempt to share it with. The mission acts as an incubator to her or his strengths as they adapt quickly to uncomfortable circumstances. The mission acts as a magnifying glass to those insecurities and weaknesses as dealing with life happens fast, and failure follows close behind. All past means of dealing with stress are left behind. Meaning we really couldn't indulge in escapism in any form. No TV, movies, music, or books. To better learn the Gospel and how to share it, a missionary turns all their attention to various forms of media centered on the Gospel. For two years, they live with a missionary companion, getting a new one every couple of months or so. Asked to stay in close proximity (within reason, of course) to them the entire duration of working together, there's little to no alone time! In short form, all comforts are stripped away, and intense exposure therapy to discomfort abounds constantly. Missions are not easy for these reasons. Keep in mind, however, they are *voluntary*. Those who decide to go on a mission do so because they chose to.

And so at 18 years old, I was assigned to the Florida Tallahassee Mission, Spanish Speaking. I went to Mexico City, Mexico, for six weeks to begin learning Spanish. After those intense weeks, it was on to my area of labor for the next two years. Those first six weeks were amazing. I forced myself to always produce results in learning the language. I consistently memorized 99+ words a day for several weeks (of which I forgot 90 of them the next day, but hey, I did what I could). For a few weeks, I had a missionary companion from Argentina who spoke no English. I excelled in learning my mission language as well as learning how the mission would be organized and its flow. By the time I left Mexico, I spoke Spanish semi-fluently, learning far more in those six weeks than in the two years I spent in an organized Spanish class. My negative, internal dialogue had produced incredible results and continued to do so as I went to Alabama to serve that community. Throughout each day, I thrived on the missionary routine. The tasks given to us missionaries, though difficult at first, became the norm quickly. I prided myself on how quickly I adjusted to my new way of living, as I lived the missionary schedule and standards as perfectly as I could.

In all of our lives, we have certain moments that stand as climaxes in our history. To list a few positive ones: graduating college, meeting the love of your life, marrying the love of your life, having your first child, finally getting hired at your dream job, and many more. Large portions of these personal turning points are, at face value, negative experiences (previously listed). Yet, to each of us, these moments are life-defining and changing. They set us on a course that initially frightens us and then steers us in a new direction. One that, up until that point, was imaginary, something of the future. Once in that moment, we recognize how our life won't be the same. Think of Jay Gatsby when he first met Daisy (The Great Gatsby - Book/Movie). His life was never as intended afterwards. Better yet, think of Stanley Yelnats getting hit in the head with that famous pair of shoes (Holes, 2003). His life immediately changed for the better after it got worse. That Sunday morning pushed me on a path I would never have taken otherwise.

Up until my personal procession hospital-bound, I had my share of hardships as a young missionary. Two minor car accidents, days of severe depression, homesickness, and the diagnosis of sciatica nerve pain at the age of 19 (prohibiting any physical movement some days). Amidst these afflictions, I met some of my dearest friends, felt immense love for the communities I served, witnessed miracles, and truly felt the personal, warm love of God for me. Times weren't all bad.

However, they were made worse by my running dialogue insisting I was a failure, weak, and fully deserving of the constant back pain. Positive experiences were only enjoyed on the exterior, never internalized. All my good work was instantly compared to an unrealistic expectation of how it could've been better and what I should've done. There was no rest between my ears. The power of negativity hung over me as I consistently chose against sharing my internal struggle, for the simple act of speaking with struggle certainly takes back the power once abdicated to a positive counterpart.

I've looked back on that passing-out experience multiple times. I've only one running theory. Mental fatigue from constant pressure, anxiety, and an inability to process emotions led to my brain shutting off. Almost like it needed troubleshooting; it needed rest. And in order to achieve that rest, it wrested itself forcefully from my controlling grasp. For so long, I had repressed all my emotions out of fear. The only other option I allowed myself was to feel numb, depressed, and constantly worried. I dove head first into perfectionism to fix all my actions that resulted in any negative emotion. I had to be perfect but let no one know that. All tasks, big or small, were micromanaged by me worse than ever. One wrong move, and I was on the receiving end of a self-induced mental screaming contest. The perfectionist inside always won because, from the start, it's all rigged, of course. Perfection remains unattainable. Self-criticism, though, is always constant.

Nobody likes a perfectionist, however, so I played the role of someone completely devoid of pressure and stress. With an outward appearance so nonchalant, I had a calming influence on the lives of many people. Making friends was easy because I was so easygoing. I knew how to be nonchalant in all the right ways, so I played that part like a multi-Oscar-winning actor. Days were had, however, when I played that role too much. I was too nonchalant, and real responsibilities were neglected. A sort of complacency washed over all notions of intentional movements towards appropriately motivated growth. I wasn't always a jerk to myself! Sometimes, I was just a bad friend who allowed mediocre effort, knowing full well I had more to give.

Can you see the oxymoronic disconnect that led to my literal downfall?

I was a nonchalant perfectionist. Wanting so badly to perform well and so badly to be accepted. Both mentalities existed simultaneously and still remain today. Rather than rejecting the perfectionism that drove success, I learned how to focus it elsewhere. Rather than removing the nonchalant within that connected well with others, I learned how to activate it when appropriate. The back-and-forth relationship of these two opposites encapsulates the resilience necessary to allow flexibility between them. The best of both worlds, hopefully. Thus, the essence of emotional resilience. And the meaning of Nonchalant Perfectionism.

Emotional resilience bridges the gap and connects the two opposing personality types. It finds the common ground within and tames both the wolves inside of you, feeding them both at the appropriate times. For the fed wolf wins the day. Protecting the innermost desire of fulfillment.

Emotional resilience weathers all troubles that boil up

from within *and* all external attacks thrown by those who have not calmed their internal wrestle.

Emotional resilience can change the tumultuous tides created by childhood trauma. Which trauma dictates our adulthood more than we know!

Emotional resilience cannot be defined as a "thing" that you buy or physically have.

Emotional resilience is a skill. A discipline. A muscle. A literal lifesaver. Life changer. And a life shaper. It is a fluid, dynamic technique developed over time.

Emotional resilience is life-productive.

Chapter 3
A New Course

The weeks following that fateful day were nothing short of rigorous. Not only did I have to cope with the constant fear of passing out again, but I also had to continue the stressful missionary work. Each mission has wonderful leaders that aid in the health and well-being of each missionary, and so they connected me with a wonderful therapist, Dr. Kim Openshaw. For the first time in my life, I spoke with a therapist. Before my mission, I felt a strong pull to seek aid from one. Yet, in classic nonchalant fashion, I purposefully put it off. In classic perfectionist fashion, I could not admit to needing help, reassuring myself that it was not necessary for me. Afterall, therapy helps those who are broken. And I wasn't broken. It took a complete nervous system override, troubleshooting, ambulance ride, hospital visit, and an entire mission organization for me to finally recognize that, in some part, I did need help.

In the very first session with Dr. Openshaw, I finally opened my eyes to the wounds inside. They had been bleeding for many, many years, plaguing my life with an incurable, seemingly eternal infection that hijacked my emotional immune system, leaving me empty. He helped me see that I could ask for help when I needed it. I began to understand that although my inner dialogue and self-criticism had produced great things, it became a detriment to my well-being. The pressure I constantly felt was placed on my shoulders by myself. Because I sourced the pressure, it was my responsibility to lift the burdens that were heavier than what my strength could bear. My eyes finally saw those wounds, and over time, they finally saw the solution.

With his help, I began intentionally listening to my inner dialogue. Rather than drown it out as a vacant sound, I heard it as a living, constant voice. It was loud. It was obnoxious. It was relentless. It was not me. Not who I really was. It reflected the opposite of my dynamic personality.

Nothing had pierced me with more fear than before the weeks in which I was tasked with giving attention to my demons and documenting their dialogue. Multiple times daily, everything stopped as I pulled out my phone to write phrases to the likes of, "You have no idea what you're doing, you're an idiot, you can't do this, sit the **** down." The fear felt was founded in the idea that writing down the phrases gave them the power to be true. Once thoughts are put on paper or the phone screen, they adopt a sort of reality. Written words approach closer to tangibility than do spoken or thought words. Physical harm only results from tangible attacks. Therefore, as these phrases obtained some level of tangibility, the perception of pain became insurmountable. And yet, I carried on with my annotation, knowing that somehow, once tangible, I'd finally be able to orchestrate ways to heal those wounds because only when brought to another level of reality can we solve these types of problems with specific methods.

After a couple of weeks of that, I learned how to rebuttal each and every thought. If you want to beat negativity, it must be met with an equal to or greater measure of *commitment to positivity*. We cannot always be positive. I know I can't, and so I don't expect that from anyone else. However, we can devote ourselves to positivity. The winner in the battle between positivity and negativity is *the one who doesn't give up*. Though incredibly cynical, if you can match that with a relentless commitment to positivity, you can change daily depression for the better. I will dig into these ideas in detail later in the book. For now, I'd like to detail another story that further cemented the need for emotional resilience in my entire being.

As detailed above, suicide ideation has had a place in my head since I was very young. Not planning on anything; I never thought it to be a serious issue. No one knew how often it was the subject of my thoughts. Part of me thought it was normal, and so I thought no more of it. The first time I distinctly remember committing myself to suicide was on my mission. Please note that operating in the role of a missionary is not what led me to suicide. Rather, it was the "pillaging pressures I put on my psyche" to prove I was a person of perfection (I Win I Lose, 2019). Looking back, there was no one instance that triggered my commitment to this matter. Pressures mounted. Feelings suppressed. Pricks were kicked against and kicked hard.

Applying what I had learned from my counselors, I called the mission nurse and expressed to her that I "didn't want to be here anymore." to her credit, she assumed I meant serving as a missionary. Many missionaries go home from their missions for a myriad of reasons, and they do so before they serve for the full, expected time. In this case, the mission president gets the call, not the mission nurse. Confused, she began telling me to call the President. Feeling deflated, I did not want to burden her with my suicide issue. "Who am I to put that on her shoulders?" I thought, "Would it not be easier to end it all to avoid all of this? Maybe if I passed out right now, I just wouldn't wake up." In that single moment of complete defeat, all I could muster was, "no...no, I mean...I...I don't want to live anymore." All the commotion between my ears suddenly eased. Like a ray of sunshine breaking through a thick morning fog, I felt a solitary, fleeting moment of darkness dispersing. Inviting this nurse in brought with it power over pain. It brought short, bursting peace. And I understood none of it.

When asked what my plan was, it sent a shock through me that I'll never forget. Like stepping into freezing water, it seized my system up. Various ideas ran through my head, and so that's what I expressed to the doctor. Having many years of an addiction to pornography before my mission, I knew how to get away with something taboo. I knew what to look out for and how to avoid detection. Knowing that, I did not detail my plan to the doctor or to myself because I knew I couldn't go the distance without somehow harming my missionary companion. Only interested in self-harm, I had the sense to expulse the idea of causing a traffic accident. Nor did I find it suitable to purposefully overdose on my antidepressants (my happy pills) and whatever mix of over-the-counter pills we had. My pain preferred a full-proof plan. A plan that was solidified just two years after that doctor visit.

On June 20th, 2021, I held a gun to my chest with my finger on the trigger. The pain had only amplified as I worked to heal, and so my pounding, heavy heart was thus ready to take a literal bullet for and from me.

Spending hours upon hours in the headspace of a suicidal person, I know what it takes to get there. I also now have an understanding of how to avoid that abyss. No person deserves to reside in that place of Hell, where there is no hope. No joy. No happiness, nothing close to contentment, and certainly not an inkling of laughter. Darkness abounds, dejection avails, and defeat dominates. Deep-seated thinking errors no longer carry a rumpus demeanor and are accepted as the norm. Death follows closely as the only companion, option, and way of pain relief. Internal destruction consequently results in external desecration of one's physical well-being. Why get out of bed if only to look failure in the mirror? Why shower if only to clean the recurring, nearly constant collection of smut and tears? Why talk with others if only to remember your social illiteracy? Why attempt hobbies if only to feel the heavy chains and demons that are devoid of any possible pleasure? Why exist if only to yearn for permanent exit? Many of us have been to Hell on Earth. We know that down there, it is no easy feat to come back to Earth. Even if for a brief, painful moment.

Though squeezed, the trigger was never pulled. I was not saved by someone finding me. I was not visited by an angel. I did not feel an outpouring of love from a higher power. I did not receive a phone call or a text. I did not have some great epiphany which magically removed my depression. I did not die, so I was not brought back to life. I stewed in that place of Hell for weeks following my proposed death day. I cannot overstate the absence of a traditional miracle that came to my rescue; it just was not there. Yet, I personally define what transpired as a miracle.

As I sat with the gun to my chest, for the first time in a very long time, I felt something. I can no better describe it than to say that I just felt that the decision about to be made was the wrong decision. No metric was given to determine *why* it was the wrong decision. To me, it was only given to know that it was incorrect. The words, "This is wrong," although quiet, pierced through the loud, riotous noises filling my head. The "right" decision was not given to me either. No clear path as to what to do next was defined. That simple, stark message was precisely what I needed.

I set the gun down and looked at it almost longingly. Almost as if I knew that I would never again visit my space in this dark, comfortable corridor. If I really wanted out, now was the time. This was the long romanticized moment. I knew allowing it to pass by would mean I could never come back to the (illusioned) comfort. All temptations to aim it once more flooded my mind, and yet they could not penetrate those three stalwart words. "This is wrong."

What followed that somber day was the aggregation of a

clear devotion to stay above Hell. Not to reach Heaven, mind you. I only had the foresight and strength to remain just above. The next part of this book I call the "How" of emotional resilience. I will take it upon myself to clearly illustrate how I've come to develop this skill and how I am *still* developing it. In my humble opinion, developing emotional resilience is paramount to successfully drudging through life.

SECTION 2

Chapter 4
How to Develop
Emotional Resilience

Passing out involuntarily was my first introduction to how much power emotions have in my life. Never before then had I ever considered that my emotions were more than just fleeting feelings. Feeling numb about my life up until that point, it made sense that I thought nothing of emotions. Gaining that awareness of my emotions ultimately heightened the potency of my inner feelings. Only after acknowledging the pain was I able to soothe the pain. This, of course, a wonderful discovery, also further juxtaposed the pain against the pleasure of life. Meaning pain was now stronger, burned hotter, and sunk deeper. Yet I'd rather live with that if I also get to experience breathtaking pleasure in spite of consistent hurt.

Attempting suicide was voluntary. I chose to attempt suicide. Even after learning of the immense joy available to me, I chose against the sacredness of life in an attempt to stop feeling bad. On one hand, I had no choice but to face the reality of my soul's pain (passing out). On the other, I decided to end all positivity, joy, and happiness because I could not justify the suffering (attempted suicide). The power of choice led me to different places in both instances. If we can choose against our life, can we not then choose in favor of our life? Forced to pass out, I chose to make myself aware of my issue. Choosing to die, I chose the easy way to stop that temporary depth of pain. The greatest ability that you or I have is to choose for ourselves. We are free agents to ourselves, and we can either play for or against life.

First and foremost, if we want to develop emotional resilience, we must choose to do so. I am not talking about an easy drive-thru order decision. Moreso, I am describing a powerful undertaking that you take upon yourself. You own it. Every facet of this choice is yours. The progress, the failure, the successes, the devotion. You adopt and take control (Willink & Babin, 2017). Recognize where you falter, admit your wrongdoings, and shine a humble, meek (see the Biblical Definition of *meekness)* light on your many strengths. Allow no person (on a screen or in person) to dictate your innermost thoughts and desires. Welcome the inevitable conflicts as opportunities to tighten the screws and become better. I could go on listing all of these vague, ill-defined phrases. But let's dive into some actual principles. Such principles can change our perspectives, life, and thought processes. Only if we allow them to, however. They will be listed as short mantras.

Consisting of three or four words, these metaphors have deep meanings that I will expound on. In so doing, I hope to provide a framework on which you can develop practical uses for them that will be specific to your life and circumstances.

Chapter 5
Emotions Are Cool

Let's finally come to terms with the fact that emotions are cool. Everything that happens in your life, all the good, bad, amazing, terrible, and mundane, are all perceived between your ears and then labeled with one of the many emotions available. Those who subscribe to the idea of emotions not meaning anything are denying an integral part of them. Others have claimed that feelings are not real and, like dreams, cannot be trusted as reality. How sad. In my personal life, some people have attempted to discredit my clinical depression. Citing that "it's all in your head!" well, yes, I'm aware of that fact. I always enjoy when they reiterate that fact, sometimes I do forget that depression isn't a wart on the back of my knee. Yet, like a wart on the back of my knee, I decide how to cultivate its healing.

In the early beginning of this development, we must give feelings their validity. If nothing else, they are at the very least ever present, every moment. They have a profound impact on our perceptions of the moment, which we, whether we like it or not, are always in. Live in the moment or remain willfully ignorant of all opportunities. We have no true escape from emotions (this can vary depending on your beliefs of the afterlife. I, for one, believe our thoughts, minds, and souls continue after death. Otherwise, you judge for yourself the escape method of suicide). Always perceiving our surroundings, our subconscious triggers emotional responses. We then have a moment to decide where we will go with how we feel. Certain situations will breed the appropriate emotion, but our circumstances cannot choose our reaction.

I will use the definition of the word "cool" and show the relation between it and emotions. Starting with cool in regards to weather, it describes conditions that are not hot, not cold, but neutral. Typically, we are on the colder side, but how we dress will ultimately determine our experience for the rest of that day. Some will be colder than others and choose to dress heavier. And some will dress completely opposite. Regardless of how one dresses on a cool day, it is completely personal. Personal preference is the key. I love cold weather. I love being cold. So, a cool day will fare me well as I dress light. My tolerance for cold weather has created my preference for colder days. Others, like my dad, hate being cold. He wants to be warm all the time. On a cool day, he will dress heavier than I do to appeal to his preferred warmth and comfort level. I hope you see the difference. Both he and I experience the same day and have two very different reactions to the day. We will be comfortable in our differing circumstances. Because he enjoys the warmth, that does not equate to my having to comply with his preferences. And vice versa. We are both validated in the choices made due to weather circumstances out of our control. I don't care that he dresses warm on a cool day; it's not my responsibility to determine how he dresses.

Drawing the parallel between a cool day and cool emotions, determining our day derives from deciding how we will dress for them. You will get cut off while driving to work. Clearly, that's an inconvenience, and anger will most likely rear its head. Much like a cool day, that was out of your control. The driver's actions are not managed by you, yet now they have a direct impact on you. Enter the cool anger. What will you do? Tailgate them? Vote them number one, give them the bird, flip them off? Curse them out? Catch up to them at the light? At the light, will you get out to get a look at them? Then taunt them to fight? How far will you let this go? I'm sure you've seen videos of those people who have done all of what I listed. They chose to let their cool anger heat up to a boil. With blood boiling, they reacted as someone who's blood is literally boiling - absolutely bonkers!

Let's say they did the exact opposite. They froze their anger. Stopped it dead in its tracks and forced it deep within. With their emotion freezer getting full, stuffing yet another emotion, they have no choice but to jettison this and all past emotions. Yet, they are not an angry person. Cool, calm, and collected. Those are all they can be and will always be. Not allowing themselves to explode, they must then implode. Depression, at times, is anger turned inward. They shut down, distance themselves from others, and begin to feel numb. With very few remedies available, these frozen emotions choke out the entry of all other emotions. Yes, this may not immediately happen from getting cut off once. But, they have been angry hundreds of times in the past and reacted in the manner described. Implosion is the only option. If they were to explode, we all know how scary that would be. We all know people like that. For many years, I was that person. I stuffed emotions, then imploded, fell into depression, and occasionally explode. An often repeated cycle.

Both responses are valid to that person's ability to respond to anger. The way it's happened in the past will dictate how it happens in the future. We truly are creatures of habit. Changing past habitual responses requires much time. Better to start soon than to never change at all.

Those reactions are both expressions of anger. Explosive and implosive. Emotions must be expressed. Do not misunderstand; I am not suggesting we learn how to live without expressing any emotion. I am suggesting we work to express emotions in a productive way. It's a cool day, so decide how you most want to experience it. Warm or cold.

You get cut off in traffic. What will you do? What I *strive* to do still doesn't come easy, yet I try to always respond in a like manner. Allow myself to sit with the anger for as long as needed. 90 seconds at most. Realize that no one got hurt (hopefully). Myself and my passengers are ok! I am still alive, well, and breathing. My truck still runs. My truck still looks dang good. I don't know that person, and they have no bearing on my day today, or life for that matter. I've got too many things planned today, and I can't allow the mistakes of strangers to derail my day. Notice that I am broadening my perspective. Naturally, it moves away from what transpired and onto important matters. The overall health of myself and others, finances (no cost on damaged vehicle), and work (tasks for the day). Perspective pointedly pushes psychoactive pressures out of your pensive playing field.

Note the personality of the decision made in both scenarios. Not one person, institution, or external force made the decision for the outlined explosion or implosion. Before the explosion took place, a clear decision was made (conscious or not) to allow it to grow. That choice is as personal as what type of coat you're going to wear on a cold day because it will affect no one else more than it affects you. If you're not careful, however, your inability to manage your emotions and the error of personal decision-making can permanently damage others. Your responsibility solely lies with you to make useful, personal decisions regarding your emotions. While it's true that we can't allow the poor decision-making of others to emotionally hurt us, we also can't allow our poor decisions to destroy the lives of others. The great "give and take" here constitutes the duality of life.

Perception and emotion processing are all personal. Which means no one else can do that for you. We are not alone in this life, but we are solitary in our heads and, thus, in our decision-making. Strap your boots. Pull up your pants. You are no special snowflake. Take responsibility for yourself. Decide how you prefer a cool day and apply the same thought to cool emotions. Reaction to them is neutral until you make the decision. It happens quickly, so start learning.

By internalizing the charge given to us to decide how we react to emotions will afford us power. With said power, we will be suited to determine in what way we will dress our cool emotions. As the adage goes, play it cool.

"Decisions determine destiny" - (Monson, 2021)-

Clearly, another definition of cool evidently shows itself here. The most common definition of cool denotes, in an informal use, satisfactory, attractive, or socially adept. A stigma exists around men and their emotions. Men are not supposed to show or even have them at times. Much like anything else not labeled cool by society, they are somewhat alienated and underappreciated. For both men and women, we need to accept the attractiveness of emotions. Because without them, life is nothing more than a dull experience. Every and each emotion is satisfactory - meeting or exceeding expectations, attractive - sought after and looked at in high regard for the lessons learned from them and the beautiful contrast they give life, and socially adapt - well accommodated for in society, appreciated, and helps us know how to navigate life.

Showing emotions is cool. Forget whatever anyone else says about it. Without showing emotion, life can only exist in a lackluster, bland, and boring shade of brown. All emotions give life vibrancy. We cannot know happiness without knowing sadness. How can we truly be happy without first being sad? Pretty cool to feel both because both give a metric to respect the other! It's attractive. So often we tailor our lives to have some sense of how we feel. We want to feel good. It's amazing to feel good. Not much more needs to be said about the cool character of positive emotions; I think most everybody can recognize that.

Let's not forget the value of feeling bad, however. At the very least, we can respect those negative emotions. Give them the value they deserve. The way they teach, instruct, guide, and offer insight is incredible! Amazing! Alluring! Breathtaking! Strong! Each description just listed describing negative emotions are the same ones used to describe a cool person. Though not commonly done, those words certainly fit the description of a cool person in your life. For the actions done by someone or something earns them the descriptive title of "cool," as it is with all our emotions.

All the while, we learn about positivity from negativity and vice versa. The yin-yang illustrates that. Black and white are so closely related, so removed from one another, and all the while a part of one another. I hope you're seeing the vitality of all emotions. Not many years ago, I ascribed myself to the school of thought which downplayed emotions. Thinking it embarrassing to show excitement, I never did. And so with it went the skill to internalize excitement. Life no longer had any invigorating qualities. Crying as a result of sadness was a sign of weakness, and I was not weak. Therefore, I did not cry. Even when all I wanted to do was cry, I stuffed those strong, sad emotions down. And so went with it the understanding of happiness. In sadness, we can understand happiness. Life changed when I saw the attractiveness of *all* emotions. I did not seek out negative feelings, but, I did not run from them either.

Let us recognize that emotions are cool. They are cool to see in others. They are cool to see in ourselves. They are socially acceptable. They are fashionable. They are attractive. Much like the cool people in our lives, we want to be around them. Learning through questions, or at least from a distance, we want to know their secret. We yearn for what they can teach us because what they have exudes the very things we desire.

Emotions are cool.

Chapter 6
Justify the Suffering

Having listened to much of what Jordan Peterson has taught over the past couple of years, nothing has had more impact on my life than these words spoken on a podcast. In an almost off-handed way, he said, "...you need to have a deep meaning in your life to offset the suffering" (Joe Rogan Experience, 2018). The impact that followed was this mantra of "justify the suffering."

Allow me to elaborate on the first word, justify, the verb of justification. Justification as a noun is either a fact/circumstance that shows a particular action to be reasonable and/or necessary. To justify is the way of finding justification for actions or beliefs. In this case, we are finding justification for life's hardships. We are intentionally creating our own circumstances that will justify our afflictions. Gratitude definitely has ground here, but this justification goes much further than a gratitude list.

Now, onto suffering. The ways in which we suffer are vastly different. From physical pain to mental, emotional, or spiritual pain, suffering takes on many forms. Life itself is full of suffering, regardless of the form. That being said, the suffering referred to in this mantra refers to the daily grind of life, with all its let-downs, heartbreaks, disappointments, frustrations, and anything that has the potential to disrupt daily happiness. I chose not to use the word 'this,' as to leave the phrase open for determining your specific suffering. Notice the subtle, evident difference between justify "this" suffering and justify "the" suffering. I'm sure, and I'd hope, as you hear or read, justify the suffering you think of a particular problem in your life. By keeping it less specific (using "the" over "this"), it allows you to decide what "the suffering" is in your life. You can determine for yourself what suffering you aim to justify. We all suffer, yes, but we all suffer personally and quietly. As personal as suffering is, the justification of such will follow that pattern. Personal justification for personal suffering.

The type of suffering I am referring to here is not the direct result of a tragic event. Though suffering clearly resides in that space, I am talking specifically about it as a whole. There are those of us who have clinical depression, chronic pain, and other lasting ailments. To one degree, we have all experienced that. Alleviation of agony abounds in positive actions done in self-awareness. How manageable persistent pain becomes with a proper vindication of life's unpleasantries.

I cannot know what your daily suffering looks or feels like.

Though I can try to sympathize or empathize when appropriate, only you truly know the depth of your discouraging feelings. You must take action to determine the specifics. Familiarize yourself with the daily fight between you and life. Sun Tzu said, "Know the enemy and know yourself; in a hundred battles you will never be in peril" (Tzu, 2005). Everyday, we battle against ourselves. As soon as your alarm goes off, it begins. Opening with opposition between hitting the snooze button or hitting your feet to the floor. Perceiving the problem, you can identify clear solutions that give you the upper hand to win that first battle. Go to bed earlier, eat more protein, slam a Red Bull to offset the lack of energy (not ideal, but effective), set goals the night before to look forward to the next day, and set your alarm earlier so you can snooze for a bit without jeopardizing your schedule, so on and so forth. In like manner, we learn our daily pain points and attach daily justification to them to make it worth the struggle.

Essentially, to justify the suffering is to take control of and revamp goal setting. Setting goals has always been a huge bore for me. It always seemed to revolve around work. Work such as completing tasks, sales quotas, and meeting deadlines. Even in school: aim for this grade, do well on this test, or study x amount of hours. These kinds of goals focused on the end result of something that did not cause the work required worth the affixed struggle. Therefore, the goal did not excite nor ignite any desire within me. Not to the fault of anybody but my own, I began to hate setting goals. Goals took on new meaning as I saw them as a way to ease the pain of suffering or at least offer meaning to it. No longer were they about a task or for a grade, rather, they were about surviving life's daily grind. You see, typically, the goals described above first focused on the desired outcome. Whereas the type of goal setting I'm outlining focuses first on the *suffering*. The mental state I was in when hearing this mantra required a complete life change. Otherwise, death would've been the answer. Hence, the amount of adjustments I aimed to make. I hurt immensely, so I had to metamorphose immensely. As you'll see, I identified specific areas as a way to pinpoint certain pain points. Below, I will illustrate how "justify the suffering" helped me and hopefully *show* it in application.

The day before I attempted to end my life, these three words came to me. For the first time in months, I felt a tiny glimmer of hope, microscopic at best. It never occurred to me that I have literal power in my life. I had the ultimate influence in determining how my life would look. In a brief moment, I envisioned a life where I felt joy on a consistent basis. I had no specific details yet, but the image of me in a happy state gave space for hope to creep in. Though I was too far gone in my thinking errors to let it deeply sink in, it went deep enough to resurface a few days after the attempt. Devoid of meaning, my life wasn't worth living. The constant suffering seemed so unjustified that my actions were incredibly useless in digging me out of my pit. Around this time, I lived in a constant state of fight or flight. I knew very well I could not win that fight; my adrenaline reserves were burning out, and soon, I could no longer stay in flight. I truly felt like I only had this one option. After deciding against my death, these words, once again, reared their head. I said to myself outloud, clearly, and sternly: "If I am to stay, I will make my life exactly as I want. I will not continue to live if I have nothing to live for."

Acting as my saving grace mantra, justify the suffering repeated itself on a minute-to-minute basis in the ensuing days. It gave structure to a formless desire for happiness. It reverse-engineered my wishful thinking for me to see how it was attainable. Searching for specific ways to add meaning to my life and make the suffering seem worthwhile kept me going.

Ultimately, the objective was not to kill myself. So, any day I could accomplish that objective was a positive. I had to find within myself any type of desire, for a desire starts the process of goal setting. So, I dug deep and forced myself to name desires of mine. Small or big, I had to determine what I could, at the least, live with. (I say live with because, at this time, I had no other desire than to die. It took various attempts to find desire. So, I started with the nonchalant "that would be cool, *I guess.*" You have to start somewhere. You have to start!) I also did not judge myself for what I wanted. Meaning if it was materialistic, I had to be okay with it because all I needed was a sliver of reason to keep moving forward. Obviously, I had boundaries and morals with which I remained. Lustful desires for sex, money, power, or mood-altering, illicit drugs weren't given room to grow. Fighting for lust, greed, or addiction does not result in true elation.

I began to list what characteristics I wanted my life to have and what I wanted it to look like. The suffering had to be made worthwhile. You see, my life *had to change* if I were to survive myself. All aspects needed revitalization. Physical, mental, emotional, and spiritual. The big four facets of life that create our lives. Literacy, maturity, and development in these areas embody *growth*. Remember, the changes wouldn't eliminate the pain. Rather, I put myself in a better position to manage.

Various goals revealed themselves, which had clear correspondence to the parts that suffered the most. I'll list them below, as well as the pain, **bolded** and *italicized*.

Defined Routine *(Lack of control)* - Consisted of:

- Working out on a daily/weekly basis *(Physical & Mental Fragility)*
- Reading worthwhile books *(Mental Weakness)*
- Regular spiritual growth *(Spiritual Indecisiveness)*
- Only *enough* leisure time *(Overabundant Procrastination)* [see Leave A Leisure Life]
- Time in creativity. *(Stagnant & Dull Mind)*
- Creative outlets/hobbies (rug tufting, outdoor activities) *(Stagnant & Dull Mind)*
- Stable income (anything would do; I just needed something) *(Feeble Finances)*
- Social circle (friends to call on when I needed them) *(Social Inadequacy)*
- New vinyl record(s) on a monthly basis *(Felt Passionless)*
- New Toyota Tacoma *(Absence of Evidence for My Hard Work)*

Every item was explicitly tied to pain. Those bolded and italicized phrases created immense longing, anger, and depression for my lack thereof. Internal pain prospered while internal pleasure pined.

However, the beauty of each one of those items shines in truth that their fruition was dependent on me! Remember, if I was to stay living, then I would make my life exactly as I wanted. The thrill of competition in achieving those goals gave me sufficient fuel to attempt it. Never shying away from a dare, I dared myself to live accordingly to justify my suffering (Danforth, 2006). Motivation slowly blossomed as my list grew. Creating an exciting cycle of new aspirations, ever so slightly, my days changed.

Microscopic hope stirred my soul. With excitement present in the thought of the life I committed to having, that hope grew. Daily perspective shifted from the pessimistic "Good God, another morning?" to the humble, "Thank you, God, for a good morning." (BlackAlicious, n.d.). Each day became an opportunity to advance further. A diverse set of long-term, short-term, and recurring goals offered small milestones to keep the excitement around. Completion of the larger goals supported efforts toward the others.

I'll provide a timeline of these goals to show how quickly things changed once I made these specific goals and implemented a few other principles.

Defined Routine - Consisted of:

- Working out on a daily/weekly basis
- Reading worthwhile books
- Regular spiritual growth
- Only enough leisure time (see A Leisure Life)
- Time in creativity.

I am really good at creating routines, like the above, and not following them. However, just one month after the attempt, I was on a consistent schedule. Though it fluctuated with how many things I achieved that day, progress was still made because of my *commitment* to the routine. I regained a level of control that had vanished.

Creative outlets/hobbies (rug tufting, outdoor activities)

- Four days after the attempt, I went backpacking in the Sawtooths with my older brother and uncle. An amazing, breathtaking trip. Offered me safe solitude for reflection.
- Four months after the attempt, I made my very first rug. Since then, I have made many, many more. I've also had the privilege of creating custom, commissioned rugs.
- Within four to nine months of the attempt, I went on various camping and backpacking excursions. Two of which were to the beautiful landscapes of Escalante, Utah. With very close friends, I enjoyed the serenity of nature.

A literal breath of fresh air allowed a dumping of headspace waste, opening room for proactive thoughts.

Stable income:

- 10 days after my suicide attempt, I got a job cleaning jobsites. In a matter of three months, they offered me a management position. A year later, I had another promotion. Though a tough job, I made more money than I ever had, which fueled my desire to continue excelling.

My finances, for the first time, felt durable.

Social circle (friends to call on when I needed them)

- Eight days after the attempt, I attended a social activity sponsored by my church. Many followed, and my circle grew slowly but surely.
- Four to five months later, I met a friend who has become one of my closest friends.
- Furthermore, my familial relationships grew stronger, from which came support, love, safety, and fun times.

Time in social settings taught me the best ways to behave socially, which acted as evidence against my insecurities.

New vinyl record(s) on a monthly basis

- One month after the attempt, I had the income to consistently grow my record collection. With little self-control, I would buy five or six a month. But hey, anything to bring a smile.

A passion for music and vinyl records bloomed, which added color to my life. And to my vinyl collection.

New Toyota Tacoma:

- Five months after the attempt, I made a down payment on a brand-new 2022 Tacoma.
- Nine months after the attempt, I drove it off the lot. Customized to my liking.

I now had a token that, to me, was a representation of the hard work I put in to better myself. On top of that, I felt capable of progressing how I wanted to in life.

Setting the above goals incited in me a desire just potent enough to get me willing to try at it for another day. I was not perfect, and I'm still not in the execution. I was only committed and *willing* to act. Truthfully, the above sights set were passionless and only put in place as a last-ditch effort. Yet, I determined what would be manageable. Going forward, I discovered other things that struck a nerve. Then, my excitement grew.

None of the above goals were set further than one year in the future. I was unable to think past just a few months because I didn't expect to live past a few days. You don't need monstrous, long-term goals to justify the suffering. Simply ask yourself repeatedly and sternly, what would make your life bearable? What would make the daily grind, daily pain worth it? You have the answer; you just need to dig. If you feel as though you can't dig, don't let what you *can't do* stop you from what you *can do*. Take a step anywhere with or without passion, motivation, or excitement. Act consistently towards something. Growth will come.

In closing, I'll add this commentary on the Serenity Prayer:

God, grant me the serenity to accept the things I cannot change, the courage to change the things I can, and the wisdom to know the difference (Niebuhr, 2021).

We are, essentially, accepting the things that cannot be changed. Yet we do not surrender all other aspects of life or our attitude to them. We accept them; we do not surrender. Acceptance over surrender.

Justify the Suffering.

Chapter 7
Commit To Fight

As a noun, 'fight' means an aggressive willingness to compete. We are competing to stay standing amidst the suffering we've justified. Though we may have found proper justification, that will not suppress the suffering. Mixed martial arts clearly illustrate the difference between justifying the suffering and then committing to fight. Those fighters have clear reasons that make the suffering worth it. Aside from loving the fight, they fight to feed their family, bring honor to their country/hometown, or personal desires for fame. Goals to make the inevitable suffering worth it. Yet, that does not take away the hits they have to take. Nor the training they have to do. The actual suffering requires they experience all it entails.

When I sold pest control door-to-door, I had a large list

of goals, aspirations, and dreams that justified the four to five months I would spend in the heat, getting yelled at, and trying to sell. I created a vision board with all my, at the time, strongest desires. Thrill of the dare coursing through me. The painful summer paled in comparison to the imagined, comfortable future I had planned for myself. I had my goals; I had my why. With the inescapable suffering justified, it was time to suffer. All that pain is worth it, right? Yet, was I *willing* to suffer? Was I willing to *fight?*

No. No, I was not. Starting the summer on fire, I quickly saw just how terrible this was going to be. I survived two months out there before I came home. The suffering was justified, trust me. Although I had goals set, they were not specific to the suffering. Even though all the discomfort made sense and had reason behind it. But, I did not commit myself to the necessary fight. The daily grind was stronger than my commitment to fighting for the sake of fighting. Some would say my why was not strong enough, and while that may be true, a strong why will not eliminate the daily grind. A strong why will certainly assist in creating incorruptible commitment, but it still needs specific attention to be fortified. Though worth it, suffering still remains. And so, we must remain. Ready to fight. Stalwart, strong, and stubborn.

The fight to which we are committed will, at times, be clearly defined and in our faces. Knocking door to door, for example, is an obstacle that's hard to miss. Either you are knocking on doors, or you are not. There are no in-betweens here, so the development of commitment to such an obvious task mimics that apparent responsibility. However, in discussing the daily grind, the fight shrouds behind life's minutiae. Because the fight hides in the gritty details of life, winning will not come easy. So, commit, be persistent, and stand aware.

Another aspect of the competition, or fight, is with ourselves in our efforts to be better than we have been. Be better than the person you saw in the mirror yesterday. Life is a race, but we are only competing with ourselves. Other people's personal striving to better themselves has little to do with you and vice versa. Developing yourself does not mean you are selfish. You are not responsible for someone's lack of self-preservation. Such an instinct demands fostering by the one who wields it. Decide today to aggressively participate in this fight of personal self-betterment. It is my belief that we are alive to better ourselves after all, which we can achieve.

The two characters that played a key role in dragging me to suicide were clinical anxiety and clinical depression. Clinical, meaning I have been diagnosed with an anxiety disorder and a depression disorder. I take antidepressants everyday, which helps with both these issues. I make the clinical distinction clear to dispel any notion that what I experience purely resides in my head and that I am weak. Furthermore, I want you to understand that I have felt paralyzing anxiety/panic attacks and the consistent work of depression to diminish my self-worth. Due to the clinical nature of these mental ailments, they are not a direct response to a temporary circumstance. No, they are always burning. Waiting to grow and consume. As such, I am to fight daily to keep them at bay. I must aggressively fight each day to stay above them. It is literally life or death for me. Because if I go as low as I was that June day, I don't know if

I'll come back. Everyday shines brightly as an opportunity for recommitment to the fight.

Another meaning of fight as a noun is - an intense verbal dispute. Inside our heads, we listen to negative and positive self-talk. Most of us aren't even aware of how negatively we talk to ourselves, meaning it holds so much power over us. Once recognized, the verbal dispute truly begins as the struggle between positive and negative grows sore. And the winner is the one who doesn't give up. I discussed this in greater detail earlier in the book. Though it always does well to reiterate the power behind awareness of the internal dialogue, it never stops. Really, the war only grows louder. Your determination for improvement must be just as strong, or stronger, than the nasty words hurled at yourself by yourself. With painstaking detail, document the damaging words. Then, rebuttal them with positivity and facts. Create tangible evidence you can refer to in order to discredit the negative thoughts.

For example:

Negative thought - "I'm lazy"

Positive rebuttal, based on tangible evidence, - "I worked out three times this week"

In like manner, the fleeting, thrown words hit no target as you maneuver yourself to a position of offense and positivity.

As a verb, "fight" means to fight against or resist strongly, to make a strenuous or labored effort, and lastly, to exert oneself continuously, vigorously, or obtrusively to gain an end. These words describe what we must do on a *daily basis* in order to achieve our desired outcome. As I've mentioned, I need to continuously make a labored effort to put an end to my addiction, depression, and anxiety. The moment I stop the fight, I can easily slip down that slope and into my grave. I can't allow that to happen. So, I commit. I'll get into the specifics later, but I will say commitment to a routine exemplifies the essential effort.

Commit means a few different things, and all definitions have application to the message of this phrase. For example, one definition is to make an investment. Regarding the fight, our time and energy are invested toward our cause to ensure we can fight. Before you enter the ring, you better have trained well enough to take a few punches and throw even more. Invest your time to get sleep, eat three meals a day, and exercise. Spend time finding activities that allow you to enter a "flow state" in which all your attention focuses on one task. Some call this being "in the zone." There are little thoughts regarding your performance of this task or about yourself. I like to think of this as doing something that is second-hand, like the dishes. The ease at which we perform this task requires no extensive scrutinizing. Success is inevitable, and gratification is immediate. Personally, I make rugs. I write. I skateboard. I read. Those are just a few examples of my flow states. Investing time, I set aside time each week for these activities. So, do yourself a favor and determine what they are. It doesn't have to be fun or creative. Long drives, cleaning, the dishes, laundry, and other household tasks offer me the same benefit.

We invest energy in prayer, meditation, and study to sharpen the mind in the verbal dispute between positivity and negativity. Time, as a resource, is very limited. We don't know how long we have left. Energy, however, is essentially limitless.

You can exhaust all your mental energy all day, everyday. And tomorrow, after a good night's rest, you'll have it back. Even if you don't sleep well, you can still artificially jumpstart the energy reserve. Therapy, counseling, or the more informal heart-to-heart conversations with loved ones are huge energy investments. In my years of therapy, I've learned it truly exhausts me to have deep, meaningful conversations. Yet, the return on investment is priceless. Those wounds I mentioned earlier were healed because of the energy investment in therapy, meditation, prayer, and personal study. Invest equal parts of time and energy in this fight.

Another meaning of commit - to confer a trust upon. Trust in a higher power to help your fight. Without my faith in my higher power, I could seldom do more than live life to the barest minimum. You may not have a faith, and that's fine. However, I would encourage you to find *something* bigger than yourself to deposit hope into. Many people refer to the "universe" as this entity. Whatever works. Simultaneously, trust in yourself that you're capable of withstanding life's blows. Trust in yourself that, in due time, you will win this fight. You are the one person you need to trust more than any family or friends. Only you spend 100% of your time with yourself, so learn how to trust yourself *to progress*. The ways other people gain our trust mimic how we must gain trust in ourselves. Others must prove themselves worthy of our confidence. Such proving takes place in their actions. It's a good thing you've got complete control over your actions. Allow room for forgiveness, trust yourself, and commit to fight. Trust that this fight ultimately is a positive force aimed at making you better.

Furthermore, 'commit' means to engage in or perform an

action. Engage in the fight; do not sit on the stands, only *reacting* to the struggle. No, *act* and be the reason for success. "Shit don't change until you get up and wipe yo' ass…" (Kendrick Lamar, n.d.). Nobody you know, although kind as can be, will fight this war for you. Take responsibility for your emotions, thoughts, and actions. Engage in this fight! Do not turn away from this course of action that, when conquered, brings you everything you want!

Lastly, as a noun - 'commitment' is the act of binding yourself, whether intellectually or emotionally, to a course of action. To have a strong fixity to something. In this case, we are bound to the fight of improving and will not move from that course of action. Don't be misunderstood either, for we are fixated on the *outcome* of the fight, not the fight itself. Fixating on the fight only would mean we stay in the fight forever. If that be the case, however, so be it. But our commitment is to fight until we feel we have reached the level in which the fight is "second hand": Binding yourself to the fight happens in the nebulous. Intangible. Borderline undefined, this action. The fight lies between your ears, intangible and nebulous. So you must take your headspace there. Change the mindset. I will list a few steps that helped me enter commitment. Setting off on this unwavering course to battle your demons is the essence of "Commit to Fight".

Steps to Commit

Step One - Bring someone into your corner.

Talk openly and unapologetically about the struggle (this struggle is what you fight against) you are having. The longer it's kept inside, the stronger it grows. Talking about it takes the power away. To commence your commitment, you will do well to bring someone onto the sidelines of your battle. While you are truly the only one capable of fighting within, your support system will give love, courage, and advice, thus strengthening your inner resolve. The day after my attempted suicide, I spoke with my parents very bluntly about my mental health. I had to. Even though I shirked from that idea. I did not want to put that stress on my parents. To be a burden to them felt worse than the pain from which I was trying to run. Bringing them into my head by hurling my inner struggle outward allowed me to get the full view of said struggle. I saw just how sore it had become. To tell your mother, "Mom, I don't want to be here anymore. I want to die. I want to leave," does something to her and to me. Her look of deep, deep care for me pierced my soul. For nothing else, I would suffer one day after the next to save her from the pain caused by my hand. Committing to the fight began with being brought back to Earth with the stark reality of the consequences of cowardly shying away from my pain.

Step Two - DO SOMETHING

All of us have felt the inner stirring of, "I *should* get off my phone. I *should* work out. I *should* eat better. I *should* do homework. I *should* do this, or do that, and not do that or this." We've all "should" on ourselves, which doesn't work. In each one of those shoulds, we know the positive outcome of each action (motive behind them, *i.e., justified suffering*), yet more often than not, we find ourselves acting out the same script day in and day out. Regardless of how often we "should" on ourselves. If you want to be committed to fight, if you want to grow better, if you want to look better, feel better, sound better, and talk better, then you have to ACT.

I believe a time and a place exists for self-love and self-care. I am sensitive, and so, at times, I need to negotiate with myself rather than pull out the whip. But! My sensitive self devours leisure more than my hard-working self strives for work. And so, most of the time, we need to summon our inner David Goggins and "STAY HARD - quote!" You want to work out, then get off your ass and work out. You have the override switch. Break loose from the chains that have kept you imprisoned in mediocracy. If you're too tired to work out, then work out tired. If you're too scared to chase your passion, then chase your passion scared! (I am terrified to write this book. I am writing it terrified. I have to because it's the only way it'll be written). If you're in too much pain to continue living everyday, then live everyday in pain. The only way to move past all of your bullshit is to physically, actually MOVE PAST ALL OF YOUR BULLSHIT. You've heard this all before, I'm sure. So now, do something about it. You know *why* you want to. It's time to get after it by taking action.

I know how it feels to wake up everyday to darkness. I know the feeling of going to bed in darkness only to wake up in darkness. And so life drags on, from darkness to darkness. I have woken up paralyzed by fear and anxiety. I have been seized upon by inner terror, which effectively tears apart all good within. I have drowned in sorrow. Drowned in depression. Drowned in degradation. Drowned in desiring death. I have been where you are, and the only way out is to commit to this fight. So please,

please commit to fight. Get up, get out, and get active. "The only way out is through..." Frost, n.d.).

Step Three - Actively discredit negative self-talk

Once commenced and you actively do something (I can't know what that something really is. It varies greatly from person to person as we desire different things. The idea here is that you've justified the suffering, and now you're taking the proper steps down that road. You are *aggregating marginal gains -* Book towards an eventual outcome. For the most part, we each desire similar things. Love, happiness, productivity, to feel good physically. And so, those are what I'll refer to), you have tangible evidence. With that in hand, you take it to those negative self-criticisms as clear proof that dismantles their argument against you. Typically, this will take place before you create a habit of positive self-talk. It's easier to work out an hour each day than it is to consistently talk positively about yourself. It is easier to act in the physical world to change your circumstances than to think your way to change physical circumstances.

"You are more likely to act yourself into feeling than feel yourself into action." Jerome Bruner - quote

Commit to fight.

Chapter 8
Enjoy Your Happiness

As I shook the dust off my stagnant heart, I panicked, not knowing how to be happy. Ever since I can remember, I have always been depressed. Depression has always accompanied me. Latched onto me like the key on the latchkey kid, sadness rarely left my side. Incapable of articulating the weight, I instead learned to mask it. And so, people knew me not as depressed but rather happy and laid back. If only they were let inside, would they see the void inside that quickly spits out deep convictions? Just a few months after turning 22, my eyes of understanding were opened. I saw the root of my addiction to pornography. The true addiction had little to do with pornography itself and everything to do with my "strivings within'- church hymnal. My emotional well-being grew a dependent on depression. I knew the proper way to function daily as a masking, depressive man. I always needed the numbing sensation depression offered me. It had become home; I fell into the belief that depression was comforting. I never wanted to leave it because it felt good! My brain rewired itself to find the quick fix of numbing out more rewarding than true dopamine and serotonin. (Scientifically, I have no idea if that's what happened. I am no expert on physiology or brain chemistry. I only know that way works to visualize the issue). And so, in order to feel the soothing sensation of numbness, I turned to pornography. I did not use to feel high, though I felt high, my goal was for the crash following the intense spike. The lasting damage of such a surge seemed to remove any possible pain down the road. This, of course, was a cyclic hell I went through. Because my personality, who I really am, never was defined by a lack of emotion. Addicts, at their core, are never really addicts. Who they are, their divine identity is diminished by the addiction that has taken away their powerful capability of proper decision-making.

Upon discovery of the root, the game changed. The fight shifted from attacking the leaves, branches, and twigs to a complete transplant, root ball, and all. For too long, I had been pruning my tree of addiction. Essentially fostering its growth! The principles I dove into above are what helped me with this transplant. Yet, as the tree was slowly removed, I found a large hole. A part of me was missing. A reason addicts stay addicts, especially after they start the road to recovery, is because they don't know how to live without their addiction. Terrified, they return to familiar forests, and relapses follow. Disposing of pornography was easy in comparison to deciding daily how deep I'd dive into my depression. You see, my depression won't go away. I've stopped trying to eradicate it for good. I just don't think that's an option, and I am ok with that. What I can choose, however, is if I will let it swamp me. Like a fire, I determine how much fuel I give it. A deep, dark ocean, and I determine how deep I dive. Deciding not to dive became easier as days passed. And yet, I was not happy. Not even a general feeling of contentedness. Not feeling happy, however, did not mean I felt sad. I know I didn't feel numb. Then it hit me. Those three words. "Enjoy Your Happiness". Like watching the sunlight break over the horizon and illuminate the landscape in that distinctive splendor and warmth, I saw *how* to feel happy.

The clear path to feeling happy revealed itself out of the obscurity of years of misinformation. For a lot of us, we are told our happiness is directly related to external circumstances. Though not told directly, almost all advertisements, in my opinion, play on our sensitivity to the search for peace and happiness. You've seen the Instagram ads claiming you've been doing something wrong your whole life. Or, you have an actor claiming their life changed after they started using one product or another. Or, you'll see another actor claiming that after they took a certain medication or used some cheaply made, highly-priced cosmetology product, they then enjoyed life more. In all instances, we are told we are not enough, don't have enough, or have been doing wrong our whole lives. Such negativity can cloud any hope of pure enjoyment of one's happiness.

To me, I saw that I must stop obsessing over happiness. Stop immediately. Forgot about being happy. Obsession over this will not produce the desired result because happiness will not be forced. Emotional resilience is about letting this obsessive trait go and internalizing happiness as it comes. (Obsession can positively affect us. Just not when we obsess over our out-of-control happiness). Our goal, not obsession, is pointed towards *joy*. Development of emotional resilience will cultivate an inner capability to have a sense of joy throughout all times in life. Yes, you will not look happy, you will not feel happy, you will not be smiling, but deep within, there's a light shining that denotes joy in the solitary fact of existing in this life. Therein lies our internal reward.

To get there will take time, lots of time. The cost of such a skill and gift requires sacrifice. Its size and grandeur merit immense responsibility and hard work. I am not there yet. However, I have come to understand that I can get there. Along the way, I will have times of happiness in the sense that I can feel its inviting warmth embrace my soul, thoughts, and overall persona. It has happened, does happen, and will happen. Yet, at every instance, you and I must let it go. Allow it entry and grant it exit. Appreciate its arrival and sanction its leaving. Enjoy your happiness, and let your happiness leave. All the while, the light of joy shines within. Joy is the mission; happiness is a plus.

Now, I will share how I've found ways to enjoy the happiness and ways which give power to my light of joy. Firstly, by defining the words of this mantra. Please note that as I talk about happiness, I am referring to those wonderful times that bless us occasionally. When practiced, these principles will ultimately help to increase our joy as well. I want to help you take full advantage of fleeting, brief, happy times.

The first word - enjoy- is primarily defined as to receive

pleasure from. The word receive, as a verb, denotes action. To the party receiving, there must be a level of action taking place in order to properly receive something. A level of acceptance is needed before proper reception happens. A level of comfort from both the giver and the receiver must be present. Meaning this, we choose whether or not we receive pleasure from anything. As the recipient, we control whether we accept or reject that pleasure. There are activities or things that are easier for us to find pleasure in than others; however, conscious of it or not, we accept or reject that pleasure. The reception of this pleasure takes place within us. We must get to a level of comfort with happiness. Its been said, "It's ok to be happy," and that's a true statement! Getting to this level of comfort can take time. Mainly, we need to allow ourselves to sit in our emotions. Remember, emotions are cool. We only control how we respond to them, as they are inescapable. Sit for a moment in clear focus on accepting the positive feelings rendered by happiness. Really feel it does require a meditation-like setting. We have far, far too many distractions these days. Above all else, our phones do little more than distract us. How can we even attempt to sit with our quiet, formidable emotions if we are constantly bombarded with news feeds, likes, and for-you pages? Shut it off, literally slide to power off. *Choose* to become comfortable with happiness and with all emotions, for that matter. A level of ease, comfort, unguarded and pressureless state of mind will set happiness deep within. Otherwise, the abounding happiness will remain aloft, out of reach. Once internalized, do not hinder its departure.

Another definition of enjoy is to have benefit from. Clearly, our happiness exists for us to benefit from. We are here to have joy. Our happiness is for our benefit, so accept it. Happiness exists outside of quantifiable restrictions. No government can strip you of this feeling. No corporate company can overload you past the point of feeling. No one person can harbor all your happiness, stockholding it over your head. Realize that. Happiness abounds, and you can tap into it! Please note the opposite here. While no other entity can take happiness from you, no other entity can offer you a lasting dose. No one else can allow yourself to be happy. Such responsibility lies only on your shoulders. Yes, we know of people, activities, music, or entertainment that can offer us doses. However, they only do so because we allow them to. You could have all material possessions, including the family and all the friends, yet remain unhappy and pessimistic. Countless stories are told of those inspiring people who, having nothing of the world, exude incredibly positive, happy lives. Please, please start benefiting from your happiness. Let it come, let it go.

Enjoy can mean taking delight in and making the most of. How often do we make the most of our happiness? In this definition, similar to receive, the word make means action on our part. Unless made the most of, happiness can come and go. Frequently, in times of trouble, we give into the "narcotic of nostalgia" (Neal A. Maxwell - talk), hoping we can relive, if for a brief moment, the happiness once past in the memories of the good ol' days. Labeling times past as "good" means, with hindsight, we saw just how good those days were. Said memories are added to our "cookie jar" from which we indulge in moments of despair (Goggins, 2021). I found that to be somewhat counterintuitive. Especially when, in the moments of the 'good ol' days', I did not feel that same happiness I presently am siphoning.

Growing up, I worked summers on my grandpa's property. Landscaping, hard labor, and really anything that needed to be done. I was trained in the school of extermination. My area of expertise. Killing gophers was, surprisingly, not how I wanted to spend my long-awaited summer. Digging for those rodents made me feel like one of them. Dirt found its way everywhere on my skin. I don't think I got tan most summers. The dirt must've stained my skin, only the smallest shade darker. From eight a.m to five p.m, I studied the ground, mapping out the intricate tunnels until I could go in for the kill. Extermination does not fall under my list of enjoyable activities. It actually doesn't fall under any list I've ever made or will make. And at the same time, I look back on those never-ending, blazing-hot summer days with a smile. They were the good ol' days. Today, I can pick out aspects of that simple job that I long for today. But what good does that do me now? Think for a moment if I had the sense to take delight in the hard work then. Would that have affected my summers? Could I look back with more fondness, knowing I worked hard and enjoyed it? Even amidst the dirt and rodents of life, we can inventory the ever-present happiness, delighting in that feeling. Thus making the most of our days in their present.

As somewhat of a passing note: to look back at days now gone is not a bad thing. So long as we do not live there. They are just that, days past. Too often, we attempt to project past happiness onto our future canvas in hopes we can get back to how it once was. That, my friends, can not be done. Surely, we learn from past experiences, which will assist us now and later; however, do not skip over the present by only looking ahead to the future. Worrying about whether we will be happy in the future leaves us in a desperate present. We can only exist in the present, and so the future yearned for never realized. "Enjoy right now, today" (Tyler, the Creator, n.d.).

Now, the word "Your" is simple yet crucial. It is of you. Once felt by you, it is in your possession. It is of yourself, for you, by you. You, my friend. YOU. Your happiness. You do not control nor own any other person's happiness besides your own! How liberating! Ultimately, another person's happiness is not your responsibility. Likewise, your happiness is not a responsibility of anyone else's. Now, do not misunderstand here; we do not go out of our way to intentionally diminish the happiness of others. Do not use your lack of responsibility over someone else's happiness as an excuse to hurt, bully, or manipulate them. We do need each other to cultivate an environment most optimal for enjoying happiness. As Christopher McCandless noted, "Happiness is only real when shared" (Into the Wild, 2007). Note who this is coming from - someone who wholeheartedly believed that solidarity would bring him peace and happiness. At the age of 24, he left for the Alaskan wilderness to live off the land. Lasting 113 days, hunters in the area found his deceased body. Alone. Lonely. Among other things found in his camp, they found "happiness is only real when shared," written in the margins of a philosophy book. An unfortunate ending to an inspiring story of actively making change. Certainly, Christopher's perspective holds credibility here.

So, while our happiness is just that, ours, it is also more fully enjoyed when shared. And we share with those we love. With all that being said, two things are true here. One: our happiness depends on ourselves. We own it. And two: we must share happiness to cultivate an environment conducive for happiness. Whether or not others choose to be happy in said environment will be determined by them. The evident dichotomy between our happiness and that of others easily gets complicated. We cannot put that personal choice *on* anyone else, and we cannot make that personal choice *for* anyone else. All the while, we are desperately hoping those with whom we interact will make the choice in the positive for happiness. If they don't, we cannot let that dampen our happy inner zone. Codependency stunts the growth of all involved. Rather than committing to make others happy, we commit to creating the culture, environment, and situation in which happiness has all the necessary makings to blossom if only nourished by the other. We each have God-given stewardship over ourselves. Use it to develop joy and enjoy happiness. Use it to help others make that choice for themselves.

That brings us to the final word here - happiness. Out of every phrase mentioned above, there is no other word harder to define. Sure, we could get into the scientific and biological meaning of happiness, but that won't do us any good. Knowing what physiological chemicals are involved in this feeling won't produce them. Knowing the reaction our body has to both serotonin and dopamine most likely will not give us that desired reaction. Countless books on this subject are out there, along with seminars, lectures, articles, essays, classes, courses, and podcasts. The book you're reading isn't much of an exception, yet I carry on. Ultimately, all these voices distract from the answer. Focusing on happiness paradoxically draws us further from it. That is because happiness, true happiness, does not manifest to you from external sources. Mind the difference between joy and happiness here. Today, we are taught by social media, the news, influencers, celebrities, corporate America, advertising agencies, and other incredible sources that we will feel better if we buy a certain product. If we buy their course, subscribe to their channel, wear what they wear, watch the movies they produce, listen to the music they make, talk the way they talk, live the way they live, and on and on and on. We lose ourselves in this "war of words," attaching to others for the answer that lies within. Attaching to evanescent, momentary material things. Reaching out to "dumb idols" (NIV, 1 Corinthians 12:2), material or otherwise, that do not offer the helping hand we seek. Very seldom can we produce any degree of joy from these ways. They may offer very, very brief happy times; however, such times will remain outside of our control.

Tactics of Application - Court Happiness, Cultivate Living Joy

Society believes happiness is joy, and joy is the same as happiness. The difference between joy and happiness has not been easy to detail, yet I hope you can see it. Ultimately, we seek internal, lasting joy. Along that way, we will find happiness, which we must take advantage of due to its short-lived duration. I will dive into certain principles that can court happiness and cultivate living joy. Along with that, these applications revolve around producing satisfaction and fulfillment.

Minimalism and Spirituality

It is little wonder why the concepts of minimalism have carved out a space in the world. The idea of adding those things that bring value to your life and cutting out the rest. An awakening has taken place, and people are feeling the weight of man-made happiness. They are now jettisoning unnecessary burdens, which in turn allows space for energy more focused on relationships and those things that elevate the quality of life. Focus changes from what I want to what I need. An approach to make things more effective rather than effectively adding more things. A simple way of life allows space for positive growth.

The idea of spirituality has also become popular. In this regard, we can thank social media for that. Though typically a cesspool for comparison and vulgarity, positive outcomes have shined through and reached millions. Spirituality denotes the recognition that we are more than human beings. We are connected to a great purpose outside of us. Whether that be a divine source (a higher power, a God) or Nature. Those who practice spirituality reach out and above rather than inward and down at themselves. Fostering deeper connections with those around them, relationships are fortified. Placing attention on something more than this human condition allows space for compassion and empathy to flow freely towards ourselves and to others.

Teachings of spirituality and minimalism derive from one recognition. That is, the worldly mentality leaves us unfulfilled. Left unfulfilled, we then seek after messages that are not popularized (probably because those messages don't move as much product as does the message that we are lesser and with this thing, we can become greater. Only to then have the cycle repeat the following year. But I digress). The essence of these unpopular messages conveys roadmaps towards happiness! The problem with happiness is a personal problem. Our personal problems are not popularized, although they are common among all! Each of us then can identify for ourselves what our happiness looks like. My purpose is only to relate my experiences to you in a way that opens new doors, perspectives, and pathways that, if you choose so, can help your efforts for a consistent feeling of content. For you, I can not determine what specific combination of ideologies, spirituality (religion), relationships, circumstances, activities, career choices, or any other detail of your life you have found that creates an environment in which happiness can easily abound and you feel it if you choose to enjoy it. I care only that you recognize the power within you to change your current, unpopular, personal problem of happiness. I only want you to take charge of it and enjoy it. I believe happiness is many different things. It's fluid. More noticeable on some days than others. It's dynamic. It belongs to you. So please, please exercise extreme ownership (over your happiness (Willink & Babin, 2017).

Steps to enjoy your happiness and your joy:

Despite not giving a definitive meaning to the word happiness, it becomes difficult to give clear steps to happiness. However, I do want to offer at least a few items that have assisted me as I work to internalize happiness. Please note: while I wish I could offer you some groundbreaking perspectives, this topic has been dissected time and time again. Meaning much of what I offer is not new. Maybe I can word them in a new way to you, and they can mean more.

First: From moment to moment, pay attention to how you are feeling.

- Emotions are always flowing. Our subconscious can pick up on cues so subtle they are incomprehensible to our conscious. As we enter into the development of emotional resilience, we would do well to consistently check in with ourselves. Be honest, search daringly, and boldly demand to bring those buried feelings to light. Only when recognized, can a problem be solved. If you want joy, first look inward, auditing all that's within you. "Set your house in order" (2 Kings 20:1). Trauma from years back, and even less intense negative emotions, can create patterned coping mechanisms that our brain follows for years. Thus creating our baseline emotional state. And for most people, unfortunately, I don't think content is the baseline. Despite all of that, "summertime always gon' come around...another smile that will lift my feet off the ground" (Fisherman, n.d.). Positive moments will come. They always do. As a sort of preventative medicine and preparatory practice, be sensitive to your feelings. So that in these sought-after, God-given summertimes, you can fully appreciate and enjoy your happiness. It all begins with being present.

Secondly, Take Stock of Outside Pressures

- Life happens. Shit happens. That's just the way it is. As much as we yearn for an easy, smooth life, we will not get it. All we can manage is our inner zone of emotional resilience. On any given day, if you are not feeling particularly cheerful, shift your attention just beyond yourself. Have you eaten enough that day? Has your workload increased exponentially? Have certain relationships been strained? Why and what can you do about it? How well did you sleep the night before? An innumerable amount of variables contribute to life's daily delight or daily disappointment. Identify variables out of your control and those within. The Serenity Prayer does well to define the relationship between in and out of control while offering a means of resolution.

The Serenity Prayer

God, grant me the serenity to accept the things I cannot change, the courage to change the things I can, and the wisdom to know the difference.

Addressing God, or a higher power, proffers us rest. Resting from stress over frail attempts to manage what you cannot will, in turn, leave courage and energy to work on the things you can change!

Thirdly, Determine if needs are met, backdropped with perspective

- Needs versus wants. An age-old battle. What do we need, and what do we want? One denotes life and death, a need. The other denotes leisure and dream, a want. I am not pitting these two against each other to say our needs are better than our wants or vice-versa. Nor am I suggesting our wants are inherently bad.

No, the feeling of desire exists neutrally. It's cool, like all emotions. The subject of desire will determine its standing. Desiring harm against yourself or others is wrong. Desiring a brand-new car is okay and can be a worthwhile goal! Likewise with our needs. Labeling dispensable items as a necessity leads to frustration. I have an old pair of headphones. They work fine, but not as well as a brand-new pair. Saying I "need" a new pair means I cannot live without it, and well, that's false. To classify desires as indispensable to our survival creates an unrestrainedness of that powerful emotion of desire. Unbridled desires, in my opinion, are found at the root of many injustices to people caused by other people. Bridling these desires strengthens us. To bridle them, we first determine which group they classify. A need, or a want. In other words, we broaden our perspective.

- Maslow's Hierarchy of Needs plainly illuminates those things we truly need for not only our survival but also our flourishment. Below, you'll see an illustration of Maslow's Hierarchy of Needs:

I'll briefly add some comments on each level to further detail needs and wants. My purpose here is not to give pages of explanation on this already well-thought-out, highly-studied philosophy. Rather, I'd like to show how it relates to us on our journey to emotional resilience.

The basic needs are the bottom two rows. Physiological and safety/security. They are the foundation, and without them, the climb to further growth steepens. For example, if you or I do not have the ability to breathe, we won't have much of a chance to progress much further, likewise, with food, water, proper sleep, and shelter. Those are true needs because, without them, we could very well die. How does this help us enjoy our happiness? A perspective broadened is a life easily appreciated.

Notice what details were left out of each basic need. Maslow, for good reason, did not clarify what type of foods we need or what brands of water are best. Nor did he say, "Designer clothes are a must, and without them, we can't grow further to self-actualization," to take that a step further, the need for shelter does not equate to a million-dollar home. In every basic need, the spectrum of satisfactory possibilities has nearly no end. I need not list every option of food, clothing, or shelter. A large, comprehensive list won't do us any good because we perceive when these needs are met immediately. The moment you're evicted and sleeping on the street, you'll know what basic needs you lack. The vast majority of people, especially in the United States, have qualifying shelters. With that shelter, chances are you've got running water and have access to food. Again, I am not saying that wanting more than what you have is inherently bad. Only when that desire boils over to a level of unbearable stress will it be a detriment.

Here is a quick example. I used to work in construction management for a custom home builder. Part of my responsibilities was to handle every warranty request inputted by the new homeowners. We built many, many one million dollar homes. On a daily basis, I interacted with every type of homeowner. Those who were very entitled; those with a huge lack of interest in getting anything done, yet complained consistently; and then those who I heard from very rarely, and when I did, they were understanding. Each house, though in appearance looked different, was essentially the same. All the same contractors worked on them, all materials were sourced from the same companies, and each project was managed by our team or even by the same project manager. The defining variable was the family that lived within the walls.

One lady, in particular, yelled over the phone as I expressed that certain issues were not covered under warranty as per the contract. These phone calls were made at least once every two weeks. I do understand the expectations you would have when purchasing a home of that caliber. However, I could feel from her tone and when I was around her that these minute issues ruined her day. You've spent time near someone unhappy. The aura conveyed in their tone, body language, and spoken word loudly shows their discontent. I cannot count how many entitled people I dealt with. The frequency was staggering enough to have a profound impact on me. I badly wanted to tell these unhappy people to regain some perspective. As the world would perceive, they had every product that marketed a "better life," and yet they expressed a worse life. I do not know all the details of their life, and as such, I don't have the right to dissect these experiences as patterns for their future or from their past. Yet, "how you do anything is how you do everything" (Beck, n.d.). It was evident to me that many of these homeowners allowed a stressful situation to get the best of them.

Now, you may be thinking, "Well, they did spend a ton of money on the house, and if there are issues, they need to be resolved. If that company can't build a good product, then they have a right to be angry. Moving and building a new house is stressful, so it's not ok to say they can't manage their emotions." The residential construction industry has many, many layers that define why some things are covered under warranty, what qualifies as broken, and on and on. For that reason, this example does have its faults. So, yes, the stress levels certainly run at an all-time high throughout the whole process. Just as with all things, there's a give and take to the relationship between two parties. And each is charged with the task of keeping in check their emotions. Those homeowners, and all people, have a right to be angry in various facets of life. The question is not about anger but rather the reaction to it. No matter how justified the anger, will it ever justify squeezing peace out from within?

Having food, shelter, clothing, water, air, and sleep can put out the fire of anger when the details regarding those needs are contested. Not *if* you have them, but what they *look like.* Aggregation of basic needs matters far more than their cosmetics. List the needs you have and acknowledge how good you have it. To gain greater looking items can be your goal, but do not let it block the simple beauty exuded from having them in the first place.

Safety and security needs are, to name a few, good health, employment, family, and social ability. Like physiological needs, the options of how they look are many. Hundreds of jobs are out there. Having one proves time again to be a blessing. Recognize the luck granted you.

Spending time with family is one of the simple joys in life. Some family lives are not as good as hoped. In that matter, we can surround ourselves with friends who will become family. See Outside Auditors section for more details on the needs of other people.

Our bodies are incredibly intricate. Millions of cells, hundreds of gallons of blood, millions of neurological connections, a heart that beats on its own, lungs fill and deflate, all body parts feel everything constantly, eyes keep themselves saturated so you can see well, the digestive system keeps things moving, an immune system always on the ready to engage, feet that support all of this, legs that mobilize us, hands intimately involved with impressive detail, arms that wrap our loved ones, and so much more. Compartmentalizing all details with good health vs bad health will take far too long. It can't be done! All of our bodies are so uniquely different, yet so uniquely similar. I do not inventory my current health problems, all the pimples, ingrown hairs, mental issues, itches, strains, aches, and sore muscles. Let's face it: because so much can go wrong, there's almost always something we can pinpoint as less than satisfactory. However, rather than listing the issues only to review them the next day, let's determine one thing. Are we on our literal deathbed? In a matter of moments, will we pass on from this life? Rarely will that answer be yes. And so, be grateful for this current breath and pray you'll have the next. Because I will only be on my deathbed once, I find it more rallying to ask myself if I can walk. Despite health struggles, can I walk? If yes, then I am functioning great! For those of us who don't have that wonderful ability, the question then becomes, am I mobile? Answered in the affirmative merits the same realization of proper functioning.

There are three other levels in this hierarchy, and their presence will be evident in other parts of this book. For now, I wanted to only focus on those two basic levels. When basic needs are met, we then have another arrow in our quiver to dismantle desires determined to derail our daily efforts for peace. Without having them met, our goals are simply to do everything in our power to get them. A process that must be undertaken with calculated efforts towards the longevity and sustainability of said needs. What I'm saying here, you've heard it before. Essentially, be grateful for what you have. Take a step deeper. Be grateful your basic needs are met. Even though you don't have Gucci slides, you're doing just fine. You are doing better than you think you are.

I wish I could give you more of a transactional formula for happiness. I wish it were more simple. Do these few things, and immense feelings of happiness are guaranteed! Life does not work that way. Unfortunate? Maybe. Ultimately beneficial? I think so. No greater lesson learned than this. How to be happy consistently. A lesson learned over a lifetime holds value above all others. A struggle? Absolutely! "Strength and struggle go together. The supreme reward of struggle is strength. Life is a battle, and the greatest joy is to overcome..." (Parlette, n.d.).

While we do have control over our reactions to emotions, that leaves much to be decided by our emotions. I have had countless times of intense, spontaneous rage for no apparent, perceivable reason. Even with a good understanding of all that I've written about, I still have bad days. And that's OK. Committing to the fight comes in here. Reminding me that despite not feeling peace, the fight rages on, and I must remain in the battle. Moments of happiness always arise, mostly spontaneous. Trusting they will come when I see no light at the end of my dark tunnel carries me on. Filled with gratitude when they finally arrive, I soak in that moment. If nothing else, I hope you can take a few principles into action so you can jumpstart that blessing. We all want to be 'happy', yet what we really want is lasting joy, which cannot be achieved with much sacrifice and time. Happiness, as a feeling, freely comes and goes. Appreciate it as you work towards joy. We want joy. We are here to have joy. As one final thought, remember that joy can be constant within. Yet happiness weaves in and out consistently.

Chapter 9
Leave the Money

The Dark Knight was an amazing iteration of the Batman story. With Heath Ledger portraying Joker, we got a glimpse into how vile of a villain Joker really is. With a run time of two hours and 32 minutes, there is no shortage of iconic scenes. In terms of script, cinematography, acting, and action, this movie delivers on all fronts. One of my favorite scenes from the movie, and arguably my favorite scenes of all time, depicts the Joker burning a mountain of cash. This is no small pile of cash; no, it's nothing short of a hill of cold, hard cash. Before he lets it all ablaze, he slides down the side in perfect Joker fashion. Soon thereafter, with gasoline poured, he nonchalantly tosses a cigar over the instantly destructive fluid. Only takes a matter of seconds before all $6.328 billion (yes, *billion* with a capital B) of his stockpile glows bright red and orange, engulfed in flames. Then follows that historical line, "It's not about the money. It's about sending a message. Everything burns" (Holmes, 2011).

Here, we have a character so vile, atrocious, and evil. Joker is many things, but at this moment, he is not greedy. If any of us had six billion dollars cash, burning it would be far from our first idea. Forced into burning it, we'd first negotiate to keep only a few million. Ok, maybe just a few hundred million, possibly a lousy billion? Then, after we get our cut, burn the rest. The Joker? The Joker took not a penny and scorched all of it. Without a second thought, every dollar was flamed out of existence.

We have hundreds of examples of real people we can learn from. Their goodness shines bright and far. Even more examples are found throughout literature of good-natured heroes partaking in sacrifices as a means to an end. Looking outside of themselves, they connect to their higher purpose. Devoted to the success of others. To name a few fictional worlds exuding heroic, good characters: Marvel, Star Wars, Lord of The Rings, Harry Potter, and most Disney movies. Joker, however, does not exemplify characteristics to mimic. He is outright evil and possibly the greatest (or worst?) villain. With that being said, bear with me as I take just one lesson from Joker that is applicable to our lives. I understand it's a movie, so there comes a point when the lines between reality and fiction are too thin to make any worthwhile comparison. Regardless, here we go!

The Joker was motivated by a purpose far greater than a desire for money. Morally wrong, yes, but powerful motivation nonetheless. I can't say Joker was happy. I really don't know. We see a sense of satisfaction within him as he makes every effort to achieve diabolical deeds. This leads me to believe he would allow nothing to obstruct him from ascertaining inner gratification. Clearly, he allowed striving after that gratification to grow out of proportion to the point of violating the lives of many, many other people. Inappropriate management of desire, in part, created, fed, and nourished the monster within, which consumed him. A paradigm shift occurred. The consequences of which are loud, invasive cruelties. The Joker found purpose in killing, instilling terror in the hearts of others, and ultimately destroying as many lives as possible. Clearly, we aren't to mimic Joker's twisted reception of satisfaction. What we can mimic, however, is the impressive ability to prioritize our desires in such a way that our own fulfillment (legal, ethical, and moral) takes precedence over desiring money.

Stepping away from the analysis of a fictional character in a fictional world, everyone wants money regardless of the problems it brings. In my eyes, money symbolically represents all materialistic desires. There exists a need for money and a desire for money (that being greed). Nowadays, these two concepts become intertwined. The line between them blurs. Clearly, we need money to live. Money is essential for nearly all parts of Maslow's hierarchy of needs. Shelter, food, living in a community, providing for one's family, and the self-confidence affixed to those successes. All of these things can be well cultivated by money, and so money in those regards is a need. Money as a want is not in itself a bad thing. It's okay to want things. We each have our hobbies and passions. Every hobby is expensive in its own right. I love collecting vinyl, which can be very expensive. The issue of wanting more comes when it dominates our every thought. So much so that we only think about ourselves and how much we have compared to what we don't have; that same comparison works its way into seeing ourselves as above others due to the things we have, so in our heads, we rank people's value based on their apparent financial status. When thoughts of money and material wealth precede all other thoughts, we begin to neglect the needs of others, emotional and physical. Remember, we are not responsible for how others feel - yet for those close to us, we do everything we can to make them comfortable out of love. There exists a level of common decency in society that, while not outwardly spoken, certainly compels us to help one another. Flooding our life, greed will rip any of these good endeavors from our hands as we can not hold onto both good and evil. We cannot serve two masters (NIV, Matthew 6:24). In this metaphor, money has an interesting duality between being necessary for the necessities and holding the capability to ruin our lives through greed. For when we exclusively focus on ourselves, we fail to connect with others. Connection with others holds a strong, potent power that pulls us out of our own heads. Once outside of ourselves, focusing on connection will heal our wounds. The desire for money, when left unchecked, will stand in direct opposition to connection. Even so, money remains one of the most sought-after things in society. Be that as it may, I maintain that we must leave it all behind to focus on higher life priorities.

The word leave means to go and depart from. In this sense, we need to go from money. Leave it and the power it has behind. Rather than fighting against its enticing pull or giving in to it, just leave it. Decide not to engage with it in the commonplace manner so prevalent today. There are two ends of the spectrum here, one that completely despises money and the other side being greed. We can't hate or love money for the aforementioned reasons, so opt out of it. Leave it behind, and don't let it mean more than it is, which is little. Money is no more than a tool. The Joker encapsulated that by burning his six billion dollars to the ground. Adding those two words, "everything burns," only further ingraining the true fragility of money. Money burns; connection does not. Stuff burns; fulfillment does not. Our association with money needs not grow more than an afterthought.

In my short life, making more money and acquiring more material possessions has, at times, shrouded every thought. The months that followed my suicide attempt, some negative energy grew within. Unrecognized at first because it was not painted as deep as the darkness I was just pulled from. I was very much reliant on myself for all my needs. At least I felt that way, and so my ego began to grow. I began believing the thoughts that I of myself, my power, my supposed wisdom, and my strength saved me from my darkness. Because I saw no physical hand of God, I forgot the role it played in my life. The logical thought process supposed that I had gotten where I was all on my own. Not only had I climbed out of darkness, but I was also making more money than I ever had in my entire life (which was noteworthy at my age, at around $50,000/year; nonetheless I allowed it to mean more than it should've). Very easily, I fell into the belief that I was *it*. I was the absolute ultimate. It was all about me that I was godlike. This overconfidence seeped into every aspect of my life. While beneficial to some degree, it ultimately left me unfulfilled. I figured if I was so great, had all this money and all these things, then why do people not reach out to me? Why do I spend nearly every night of the week alone? No friends, no girlfriend, no close relationships. I had no answers to these questions other than it was their loss for not reaching out or hanging out. I built up walls against needing connections to justify my lack thereof. Which lack was because of my very own actions. Yet I believed I was too perfect for that to be the case. I hope you can clearly see the web of lies I created for myself. The want of money and material only further entrapped me in my own web.

I failed to recognize how little power I actually had. My pride got in the way of believing in my higher power to the point where I stopped striving for His guidance. And so I found myself constantly judging people as a way to make my insecurities disappear. As I went to work, I would judge other cars on the road, how the people inside dressed, and compare them to me - with me always being the better of the two. I judged how people acted, how they spoke, and what they said; I judged every little thing about everyone in my life - always putting them below me. When my thoughts weren't occupied with judgments, they were fixated on how much money I was making, what I was going to buy next, and what I could buy for my girlfriend at the time (somehow, I managed to get a girlfriend), so she liked me more. My whole mindset went from "I don't want to live" to "living is alright if I am better than everyone, if I am a god." Greed took over, and I thought little of the needs of others. In regular conversation, I found myself drifting away in thought, followed by contempt for that person. Only when talking about myself, my image, my life, and my interests did I perk up. I really had little common decency for anyone but myself. I was conceited with a blown-up ego and a love for money. I started catching on to all this when I would see how others reacted to things I'd say. I'd see the annoyance in their eyes. Happening time and time again, I finally stopped thinking it was them and turned my magnifying glass of judgment on myself. I would listen to my thoughts as people spoke to me. There were some heavy disconnects going on there, and it wasn't until I looked at myself that I saw my pRIDe (notice how within the word pride, the word "RID" is clearly spelled out. Rid meaning to make free of), and it was ugly. I was truly appalled at the sort of things I was thinking. I hated how quickly I would chew others up and spit them out in my mind. Man, in my head, I was the biggest douchebag there ever was, and it was seeping into how I was acting, as it always does. Not only was I distancing myself from others, but I was also moving farther away from God. In so doing, I lost all the benefits of being close to my high power. Every aspect of my life was significantly more difficult without consistently involving God.

A quick note on pride. My religious background defines pride as the source of disconnection from God. (Proverbs 11:2 "When pride comes, then comes disgrace, but with humility comes wisdom." Proverbs 16:5: "The Lord detests all the proud of heart. Be sure of this: They will not go unpunished." Proverbs 16:18: "Pride goes before destruction, a haughty spirit before a fall. Holy Bible, ESV). Pride puts itself above everyone else, suggesting that no assistance is needed. The pride I reference borders conceit and arrogance. Which differs from feeling a reverence for one's own accomplishments. One type of pride will say, "I did it all on my own, with no help," and the other will say,

"With all of the help, it was done." One praises personally before praising others. The other praises others before praising oneself.

At this time, I still attended an Addiction Recovery Program meeting, essentially an Alcoholics Anonymous meeting, which only centered more around God and Jesus Christ; though my attendance was shallow at best, I went. In the sharing portion of the meeting, I sat listening to other addicts share their stories, and I tore each of them apart in the back of my head. At this point, it was automatic. To this day, I am not sure what instigated this mental, tonal shift. God helped, and also my honest observing actions of others. I speculate I moved far enough from who I really was that I finally felt the effects of the broken connection. And so, I began to self-reflect. Which always seems to be the first step amidst the turmoil. See what you are doing compared to what was done in the past that created peace. The stark difference will be clear. Look inward, set things in order, then reach out to others. Quickly, I saw the mess I made. And it hit me. It all came crashing down in my head with those three words. Leave the Money.

Immediately, I saw how my pride grew with my income. I began to see the root of my judgments and contempt. It was all based on money and material possessions! I had been blessed beyond measure being pulled out of darkness to then be given an amazing job, and all I had to thank was myself! How selfish! How short-sided! My needs were more than met, so I went to dance with greed, and together, we stepped over every good thing.

Now, this book serves no purpose adjacent to financial techniques, tips, or tricks. However, I will include a few practical methods in our efforts to leave the money behind. Yet, I am no Dave Ramsey. So, please do not adopt my small methods as the path out of debt! I only include this because of the influence greed has over our daily well-being. Remember, the primary goal is to curb these potentially devastating desires.

To leave the money, I had to first change my spending habits. I made a budget, which literally is the simplest thing one can do to prevent a detrimental lifestyle! As soon as my paycheck hit my checking account, it left! I paid off all bills immediately. I determined that I could save close to 30% of each paycheck, and be left with enough for food, gas, etc... I even had enough for one or two vinyls a month! I disassociated myself from a restrictive budget that left no room for me to enjoy what I enjoyed. I disassociated myself from a loose budget that left me with barely any money to buy groceries for the month. I left the love for material possessions behind. I opted out of believing money mattered more than it actually did. Subsequently, I opted out of believing my status was based on what I had, AND I opted out of believing that my status mattered. I knew then, and know now, that I am of immense worth for who I am, undeterred by numbers in the bank account, by numbers on a screen. I chose to leave it all behind. I left it all behind to pursue a happier, kinder lifestyle. I left it all behind to grow closer to others. Relationships always matter more than money. I tightened the few screws that came loose over a time of low maintenance. Made simple changes quickly. Making changes happen faster than holistically changing.

Money was catalytic to the growth of pride and greed. Which pride kept me from growing closer to God. My pride made life harder, so rather than chop away at the branches of pride, I went to its root. And for me, it's money. Ultimately, the idea behind leaving the money has little to do with money itself. It's about shedding pride away from our lives. Shed pride and cultivate humility. Be humble, grateful, and attentive. Realize everything in life is given, seldom earned, and give thanks to God for giving it. Or, give thanks to your higher power. At the very least, to the universe. See, I chose the word money because I believe for many people, possessions lead to pride. The idea pride plants in our heads is that we did it all on our own, so we forget God and all the details and variables that played a part in our successes. In other reason, the recipe gives us all we have. To rid pride from our lives, we must root out its source.

I believe the vast majority of us are not like the Joker. We don't find satisfaction in the destruction of others. It is my belief that we humans are generally good! We all want the same things. Whether Apple or Samsung, we just want to connect with our loved ones in the most accessible way possible. To feel loved, supported, connected, cherished, safe, and at peace is universal among all people, all races, and all cultures. Republican or Democrat, we just want our voices heard. We're all made of the same stuff and are susceptible to similar vices. My plea for us is that we can allow our good desires to overshadow the covetous channels of greed.

The majority of us find true, simple satisfaction from good deeds. Often an inconvenience, we can feel the warmth from service to others. Helping one another. Stranger or friend. Building closer relationships, friends or strangers. Inventory those worthwhile feelings and seek after positive passion. Burn the pile of six billion dollars if you have to. Turn your back to those flames and press forward to a life uninterrupted by greed's nasty claws.

Leave the money.

Chapter 10
68 Hot, 68 Cold

When heating your home, you can heat it to 68 degrees, probably when it's cold outside. You can also cool the house to 68 degrees when it's hot outside. Both are set at 68 degrees; however, there are two versions of the same temperature. 68 *hot* 68 *cold*. Much of the difference felt comes from your perception of that temperature. Live with anybody for an extended period of time, and this becomes self-evident, fast. The truth remains that you can experience both sides of this temperature. 68 degrees is 68 degrees. Still, 68 has two sides. Hot and Cold.

A US quarter is worth $0.25. One side, considered "heads," has an etching of George Washington. The flip side, known as "tails," varies in design as all 50 states in the continental US have something to represent their state. From horses to a space shuttle, these coins have got everything. Each quarter, regardless of design, still holds that same $0.25 value. Although in our hearts, we here in Idaho would assuredly affirm that our quarter is at least worth $0.30, but that's neither here nor there. One quarter, two very different sides. Heads and Tails. Same value.

A quarter and 68 degrees exist regardless of how they vary in that existence. The same goes for us and our emotions. See *Emotions Are Cool*. Emotions exist as they are, and we determine if they will be hot or cold. Heads or tails. Good or Bad. Productive or unproductive.

There was a time in my life when this principle rang very loudly and very true. I was in a wonderful relationship with a beautiful girl who I loved. The time we spent together will always be looked upon fondly. One day, seemingly out of the blue, she felt we had to break up. As she told me this, I did the only real option I had. I honored what she felt to be true, and out of love, I let her go. The weeks and months following that day were clouded with a depression that I had not interacted with since the suicide attempt. Triggered by this loss and caught off guard, the depression bug bit. And it a bit hard. With its teeth already sunken in, it felt as though it found a way to further puncture whatever resilience I built to the pain. For a brief moment, I gave way to the enticing warmth of my smoldering fire. Growing into deep orange flames, I now found myself engulfed in a new reality of loneliness.

Knowing the principles I have written about in this book helped. Still, and always the same, I had to put them into action. Determine what would justify the suffering of this break up, essentially, how I would live the single life. Moments of happiness were few and far between but occasionally present nonetheless. I committed myself to fight against the raging flame as I worked to regain control. Eventually, painstakingly and out of breath, the day finally came when I stabilized to my regular level of emotional state.

Near that long-awaited day, I had the idea of 68 Hot, 68 Cold. Much like the breakup, it hit me out of the blue. See, my depression behaves similarly to that quarter or those 68 degrees. Meaning I can decide on which end of the depression spectrum I will sit. There is a productive depression and an unproductive depression.

Throughout those painful weeks, I still lifted weights at least three times a week. I still did my cold plunge two or three, sometimes four times a week. Having started a new job, I made an effort to associate myself with my coworkers. Who, nowadays, make the workplace an enjoyment rather than a burden. I attended my religious meetings and asked for a blessing from leaders. Played soccer at least once a week. I wrote a few sections of this book during that particular rough time (arguably some of my best writing). I kept my ecclesiastical responsibilities, which always centered on serving other people. Determining their needs and doing what I can to meet them. I was still social, hanging out with friends, and I made feeble attempts to make new ones. Kept in touch with my parents, seeing them as often as schedules would permit. I would argue that all those things I did are what some would suggest are the ways to stop being depressed. However, I was depressed before I did any of those activities, during and after. Be that as it may, I could've done the complete opposite. Only further entrapping me in chains of depression.

Before the suicide attempt, this is how I would've handled the breakup. I would isolate myself every chance I got. Go to work and isolate there. Eat lunch by myself and speak to others only when absolutely necessary. Lunch would be the only meal I'd eat. After work, it would be me alone, wasting away, pinning for what once was. I would've spent hours indulging in pornography. Soon, all my thoughts would be objectifying all women. My current friends would not have heard from me for weeks on end. The same goes for my parents. Rarely would they see me or hear from me. The gym? Forget it; I'd be too busy scrolling on Instagram, Facebook, and Reddit to have time for the gym. No cold plunge, no soccer. All passion projects would come to a halt, and this book thrown the farthest out the window. Ecclesiastic responsibilities not meant, people not helped. Religious worshiping intended for my strength would cease entirely. In my own head, I would live, and in my own head, I would never leave. I would have spiraled further into depression. In doing so, the negative self-talk would shoot at me constantly. I'd have no ammo with which to fight back. Inactivity gives depression ammunition. Growing in attractiveness, suicide would have seemed like the best and only option.

Even though I remained depressed in/after productivity, I trudged through that swamp at a much quicker pace and for a lesser distance otherwise. All I felt was depression. All I felt was darkness. But why would I give myself atrophy when I could prevent it? Despite the darkness of the tunnel, the light shines still. I am not going to suggest to you that your depression will go away when you cold plunge three times a week. Truth is it won't, clinical or otherwise. It will, however, offer you at least a few minutes of rest. It will rest your mind from focusing on the negative. I will not suggest that exercising will stop the pain. What it will do is provide tangible evidence against the negative self-talk. You will harbor all ammunition needed to fire back at the constant barrage of self-destruction.

Understand that all those activities I still participated in were not done happily. Occasionally, I would find moments of happiness in each of them, but for the most part, *I did not want to be productive.* Don't be mistaken in your perception of me as I dealt with this hard time. I could not force a genuine smile. In the moment the door to my bedroom closed at the end of the day, tears would flow. I was not overly positive. Actually, I just wasn't positive! Overly or under-ly positive. Each morning, my eyes opened, and immediately, the battle ensued. In every case listed above, I went through the motions until whatever task was accomplished.

Undeterred by the pain within, we allow strength (emotional and physical) to grow as opposed to giving in. The greatest benefit of productive depression is not falling further into the unforgiving pit of darkness that lies adjacent to hell itself. I have been there before. No one deserves to be there, and everyone can actively further themselves from that place. It does no good to do no good. It helps nothing to help nothing. So, help yourself. The power, decision, strength, effort, success, and victory are yours.

Accept the Temperature

You will not feel happy all of the time. You will have occasion to ask or scream (whichever comes first), "Why? Why me? Why now? What is this all for? Why is this so hard! Why can't this pain end? What have I done to deserve this? WHY, WHY, WHY!" Everyday for months, these were the words of my every thought. Center stage or not, these questions found their way to the PA system of my inner dialogue. Many private moments were had in which I spoke them audibly. Anger grew as I received no answer to those questions. Sure, I had theories. But theories do little to soothe deep wounds. Alone in my anger. Alone in my confusion. Alone in desperation for a sliver of light. Finally, I had had enough. After 30 days or so of constant questioning, I asked myself sternly, "What benefit do these questions have? If you knew why she left, would she come back? What will you do if all these answers come now? Are you not tired of this? Can we (*In my head, saying We help bring two opposing thought processes together*) not have a moment of rest from constant interrogation?" Rather than question the source of the problem, I questioned *how* to solve the problem, regardless of the source. One question sunk deep, "Can we not just accept the temperature and move on? Can we not just *accept the temperature*?"

Having wrestled emotionally for many days, all the energy I had was lost as if I were a boxer in the 12th round. All second winds and adrenaline were gone. Left to swing weakly at my problems, I could no longer stand. Brought to that point, only then was I willing to accept the temperature. It took all my energy to give in and let go. So badly, I hoped to stand strong and make changes to my circumstances, which can be done when you are the only party involved but involve just one other person, and you must account for their free will. Life abased me, and I had no choice but to accept.

In that letting go of power, I found a sense of peace falling over me. Fear of losing the illusioned control I thought I had kept me from allowing the higher power to take over. I had to give my pains, fears, worries, and anxieties to my God. And much like an ice bath or cold plunge, I sat in that cold water, accepting the temperature in an attempt to learn from it. You've noticed how often I talk about cold plunges. I believe they have been crucial in my emotional development, and for good reason. The first 30 seconds in 39-degree water is awful. As you acclimate to your cold reality, however, in the next three to five minutes, a type of silence falls over the mind. Focusing on your breathing, only the immediate problem of cold water can be addressed. Rather than running from the problem, you breathe through it. The best sessions I've done have been when my alarm goes off; it surprises me. After acceptance and acclimation, acknowledgment abounds. Acknowledging the trial at hand to be only a small moment. It all changes after three minutes. Acknowledging that I can get through this. Acknowledging that I can't change the circumstances. Acknowledgment of the lessons available to learn from. Once accepted, the temperature of our trials become bearable. Once bearable, we then move on to better times. We are stronger. We are now more capable of carrying higher capacity challenges. We start warming up.

Oftentimes, life skillfully brings us to our knees, and out of desperation, we, with great exhaustion, hang our heads, hoping soon the wave of trial will pass us over. We know this. We know that our trials will soon exhaust all our energy till we have nothing left to throw. No strength, tactics, or new principles. To accept the temperature is to set in motion this surrender with the leftover strength. Rather than fight, use your power to surrender.

Control the Smolder

Within each of us lives a fire. A fire that, when cared for properly, is used to our benefit, much like the combustion that drives our cars or the heat that warms our homes. However, when handled undisciplined, a forest fire rages. Destroying the beautiful landscape within each of us. Our inner flame warms both the positive and negative, depending on how we feed it. Much like the two wolves, the fire can devour or lead to devotion. Either felt as burning passion or burning apathy. Such a power demands an equal level of management.

As my mental health began to stabilize after that suicidal summer, I was feeling good. I enjoyed life, sought opportunities to grow, made new friends, and strengthened current relationships. I got promoted at work, and in my church, I got an important assignment to help the missionaries; around this time, I made a deposit on a car that had been my goal for years, and so many more good things. My life was becoming what I wanted it to be. I felt as if I couldn't have made it to that high point in my life without first having gone to the lowest rock bottom. I was, and am, appreciative of my own personal hell, which highlighted my heaven. I remember sitting in a class discussing mental health. Specifically anxiety and depression, as those two are common these days. A girl told about her struggles with depression and how many days it stopped her from getting out of bed. Those days would turn into weeks, and she felt powerless against the depressive paralysis. I was all too familiar with the paralysis she described, as I, too, had similar symptoms. Yet I knew that the powerlessness was a product of her own mind. In all my depressive bouts, they became far less severe the moment I stopped giving fuel to the fire. Then these words came to my mind: control the smolder.

Having been diagnosed with depression, I will always have it. I know that no matter how many conversations I have with myself, no matter how many friends I have, no matter how many vinyls I collect, I will always have this depression. I don't know why it is a part of me, but it most certainly is. Therefore, I cannot allow it to grow more than just a smolder. I know that when I let it grow bigger, it has the power to kill me. Literally. As it has already almost done. We, each of us, have the power to determine the size of our individual smoldering fires. Mine is depression; it's always there. Smoldering and wanting to grow. Yet I control it. I decide if I will allow self-pity, guilt, resentment, fear, or loneliness to be kindling to the smolder. Those negative thoughts/emotions are the kindling that takes a smolder to a small fire. The emotions/actions that come as a result of those thoughts are the larger pieces of wood that fire needs to grow larger and larger until it kills. Knowing the smolder is ready to eat, I have to be very self-aware of how I'm feeling. I used to consistently check in with myself to make sure I was doing okay, and was happy. Soon, however, I realized always asking if I was happy got in the way of just being happy. These days, my regulation of emotions is almost automatic. Though I feel the warm, familiar pull of the smolder, I understand it will only provide warmth for a short time before I cannot bear the heat. While always there, I do not allow it to have the power it wants. I am in control. Understand it requires help from many different positives. Family, friends, connecting with others, enjoying hobbies, laughing, music, etc. All these things help me to regulate the amount of available kindling. Out of all those things, there is no better way to live than having a constant relationship with God and Jesus Christ. Above all things, their love upholds me. I am no saint with my emotions, just humble enough to accept the help God gives me.

Everything is internal. In every interaction in life, we decide how we are to react. We decide how we will perceive everything. Perception is life. How you perceive life's daily grind will determine the size of your fire. Will it be a smolder? Or a bonfire? A raging forest fire? There's a positive twist to this as well, you know. Will you add fuel to your competitive fire, which drives you to succeed? Will you add fuel to your fiery passions in pursuit of the masterpiece of your life? My friends, you are in control. Always remember that. No one adds fuel to your fire other than yourself. No one can make me depressed; no one can take me down into that hell other than myself. The smolder I control is that of depression. Unchecked and uncontrolled, it wields the capability of killing me.

As a final thought on this topic, I love what Daniel Johnston says in his song "Don't Let the Sun Go Down on Your Grievances," he sings, "Do yourself a favor and become your own savior" (Johnston, n.d.). I don't think Daniel suggests in this song that we can save ourselves in religious and afterlife terms. No, I believe Daniel points out that we are the ones who will save ourselves from our fires. You are your own savior in that you decide if you'll be angry, happy, sad, joyful, or depressed. You can not rely on others to regulate your emotions. You and only you are responsible for your daily happiness. Become your own savior by controlling the smolder. I don't know how else to get his message across or how to further put this idea into words. You have the power. You control the smolder. You enjoy happiness, or you don't, at your own discretion. We all need to learn this, and I still am. Almost every day, I have to remind myself that I can not add fuel to my smolder by drowning in thoughts of self-pity and self-doubt. I know where it leads, and I have too much potential to accept an early grave. Your smolder may not be life and death. But you know your vices. You know yourself enough to determine those things that need regulation. If you don't know, you can learn! You *can* know because you are in control of your own emotions, smolder, destiny, joy, and life.

The following weeks after that break-up, I did not regulate my smolder all that well. I added everything from kindling to large logs to my fire. Self-pity, anger, shame, resentment, all negative emotions fueled this growing fire. A familiar warmth engulfed my tear-filled eyes as I sat once again admiring the depression's bonfire within. And still, I knew it was not right, not productive to sit idly by allowing the fire to consume. I gave it fuel, and I could just as easily stop fueling it. The principles listed above allowed me to choke it out and remove its source of power. Until finally, I regained stable control over the smolder and moved on.

Control the smolder, accept the temperature of life's circumstances, and decide if you'll live in 68 hot or 68 cold.

Chapter 11
Outside Auditors

Despite my best efforts to be a lone wolf like Rambo, Master Chief, or the Green Arrow, I can't operate on my own. I get trapped inside my head. I spiral out of control quickly and fall in deep. There's always traffic in my head. Each car plays something different. From music to podcasts to audiobooks, rarely do I hear quiet. There are loud diesel trucks, silent electric cars, and, of course, the souped-up, straight-piped Honda Civic. Nearly endless amounts of varieties. Size, make, model, color, year, driver and passenger inside, their conversations, dogs with heads out the window, and on and on. It seems when I focus too much on the traffic, that's when all the lights turn red. The flow stops entirely, and the road rage syndrome takes hold. Anxiety, anger, and angst are what follows. A few of the more belligerent drivers slam on the gas and brakes at the same time. Causing me to feel like I've got somewhere to be and no means to get there. A type of paralysis takes over, and the smoke from the burnt rubber clouds my vision. It has gone on too long, gone unchecked, and soon, that anger turns inward and into depression. The spiraling has begun. The whole transformation process, depending on the day, can take just a few minutes. Much like rush hour traffic and only red lights don't mix well, complete solidarity and I don't get along as I'd like them to.

I've found that interacting with friends changes the red lights to green. The traffic in my skull moves with a single green light. As I connect with others, more green lights turn. Next thing I know, I feel the relief of each driver to finally go, at the very least, the speed limit and onward to a better place. I am not saying that in order for traffic to flow, I need to have deep conversations with others all the time. No, even laughing with coworkers offers enough relief to keep things moving. Deep conversations with family, significant others, closer friends, and therapists will certainly expedite the process. At times, a new traffic pattern will emerge along with further healing.

We all have our circle of influence. For my purposes, I am referring to those with whom we interact on a daily basis. Because there are more strangers than we have close relationships, our circle is broad. It includes but is not limited to, coworkers, clients, customers, managers, cashiers, people at the gas station, others at the grocery store, social events, and so on. We've all got a chance to influence everyone we see in a small way. Brief interactions with those on the outskirts of our circle have the potential to assist us in getting out of our own heads. We benefit from at least being willing for the outskirt people to draw in closer. All relationships begin with people interacting with others that exist far from us. Welcome those brief, unplanned moments that can put a smile on someone else's face and your own.

As the circle tightens, we zone in on the people with whom we confide. Our loved ones (close friends included) create the Tight Circle. These are the ones who we call when we feel lonely. The ones we ask for the help no one can provide. The ones we are comfortable giving a glimpse of the head traffic. The members of the Tight Circle are our outside auditors. We convey our desires, disappointments, and dreams to them. Knowing us well, they discern from our need to vent and our need for advice. A degree from an accredited university is not a requirement for a listening ear. Nor does it take the place of one's unique life experience. And so, this Tight Circle becomes a place of refuge. My mom has got to be the leading member of my auditing team; I mean, she's always there for me. Growing up, and still to this day, when I say, "Mom, I've been thinking..", typically followed by an idea that makes a wet napkin seem useful, she always replies, "Uh-oh...". The lighthearted reply of "uh-oh" brought laughter and made talking about everything going on much easier.

Keep a tight circle of people you let inside in order to allow you to grow outward and upward. The interruption of connecting with those of your Tight Circle will do wonders for you. Especially when seemingly everything in your life breaks loose, you'll need this group's support.

More beneficial than having a Tight Circle is participation within it. This privilege is only maintained by you being that one friend. Offering your hand and your ear when needed. At times, you may have to take the first step, initiating a conversation of connection that could create lasting camaraderie. In which case, though uncomfortable, growth for you is assured. Said the best from the Bible, "For whosoever will save his life shall lose it: but whosoever will lose his life for [Christ's] sake, the same shall save it." (KJV, Luke 9:24). Believe what you will about Jesus Christ, but clearly He devoted Himself to serving those around Him. Surely, to lose our lives for His sake is to be of service to those around us as that was His purpose, His sake. True friendship with those you love extends beyond any particular religious affiliation. Create these relationships by being the type of friend you wish you had. Maintain these relationships by being the type of friend you wish you had.

To continue the traffic analogy, more often than not, I forget there are lanes of traffic headed in the opposite direction. Trapped alone inside my traffic-flooded head, I rarely look outside of my field of vision to those others who need my help. Certainly, with the assistance of others, all our lights turn green as we turn our focus to lifting others. (Now, here, the traffic analogy breaks somewhat. When stuck in real traffic, do not completely disregard your lane because you change your focus. Obviously, drive responsibly). For our purposes here in discussion about our outside auditors, we will benefit the most from supporting others. Yes, there are times when we need to pull our tight circle close around us. Do so as needed, and remain close as an outside auditor when *you* are needed. I promise *you* are needed.

The philosopher Alan Watts married philosophies together to create his own unique way of thinking about the world. In recent years, audio recordings of him have been added as intros to songs, which invoke almost a nostalgic, reflecting feeling. He certainly had a way of provoking inner motivation towards greater accomplishments. Writing more than 25 books, he interpreted many Eastern traditions of Buddhism, Taoism, and Hinduism for those of the Western world. His influence has proved long-lasting. In closing, allow me to share a quote by him, "A person who thinks all the time has nothing to think about except thoughts. So, he loses touch with reality and lives in a world of illusions" (Watts, n.d.). Evidently, interaction with outside auditors in the tight circle pulls back to reality. Only when, in reality, can we properly make needed changes for advancement.

Chapter 12
Leave A Leisure Life

As one of my many influences, Alan Watts has many, many quotes that have struck me deeply. I can't help but try to convey his message in a new way for a new audience. So, allow me to share another quote from Alan Watts that will introduce this next section.

"Now I know the word discipline isn't very popular these days. And I would like to have a new word for it because most people who teach disciplines don't teach them very well. They teach it with a kind of violence. As if discipline was something that is going to be extremely unpleasant and you're going to have to put up with. But that's not the real secret of discipline. I would prefer to use the word skill. Discipline is a way of expression. Say, when you want to express your feelings in stone. Now, stone doesn't give way very easily. It's tough stuff, and so you have to learn the skill of the discipline of the sculptor in order to express yourself in stone, and so in every other way whatever you do, you require a skill, and it's enormously important for people to understand that *there is absolutely no possibility of having any pleasure in life at all without skill.* (italics added)"

Emotional maturity, emotional intelligence, and emotional resilience are skills. Skills that, when developed, lead to a productive life. A pleasurable life. Discipline, too, is a skill. Those two words are synonymous in this regard, as Alan points out. I will interchange these two words throughout this next session. While they vary slightly, given the context, they are still very similar. This truth reveals itself in various aspects of life. I will turn to sports to demonstrate how skill, or discipline, is a requirement for full pleasure.

One of the most popular games across the globe is soccer, or football, for those of you who care. Each match runs 90 minutes. Few stoppages and sometimes fewer goals scored. For this reason, many onlookers call it boring. I love soccer, and I have to agree with them. Some of those games take too long! But I digress. Before the 90-minute match, there were hours and hours of practice given from each member of the team. Drills were run, weights lifted, goals scored, goals missed, formations perfected, shooting forms corrected, team chemistry refined, proper equipment received, injuries recovered from, and more. Each individual on the team must pull from within their discipline to practice. Not only to show up but to work harder than planned when the game starts. They must be in the right position, handle the ball well, keep it from the opposing team, make reliable passes to teammates, trust in their instincts (which were born from practice and sharpened by discipline), and thus become an asset to the team. If all of the team honors the responsibility affixed with being on the team, then beautiful goals are scored. Ultimate satisfaction follows, as does great pleasure. In other words, the outcome of discipline/skill.

Even in solo sports like wrestling, golf, skateboarding, bowling, surfing, skiing, or snowboarding, the best pleasure comes as the result of hours of disciplined practice to create the skillful techniques necessary for the highlight reels. The greatest pleasure in all of these sports comes after the proper dexterity is paid for in time and energy. That pleasure requires skill/discipline.

The game of life requires the same amount of rigorous training if we are to take pleasure from it. We've got to put the work in. Every activity, in my opinion, takes work. To one degree or another, we are working even when we are not "at work." The deciding factor between work and play resides in the reason why we are engaging in the activity. We got to work to make an income. We make an income so we can pay for the necessities in life and also pay to play. We play in thousands of different ways, and ideally, we work so that we may live, rather than the degrading circumstances of living that we may go to work. Obviously, we seek for the play in life far more than work. On this note, Alan Watts says, "Don't make a distinction between work and play. Regard everything that you are doing as play, and don't imagine for one minute that you've got to be serious about it" (Watts, n.d). Adopting this mentality will make the arduous daily tasks of life more enjoyable. Play, in this regard, is what we do when we are fully enjoying ourselves. If we can make a game out of our daily work, we are then *playing* the work rather than *working* the work. Even more highlighted this idea when he suggested we don't act seriously. A bit of lightheartedness can go a long way. Work and play are one and the same, if we can see them as such.

Without disparaging the legacy he left behind, I'd like to offer a differing opinion to the idea of turning all work into play. I'd like to add a different perspective, which has been instrumental in unlocking my mind for productivity.

If all our work becomes our play, then the reverse is also true. Our play becomes our work. One in the same, indistinguishable from one another. Take a moment to recount all the steps taken in preparation for one of your hobbies. As an example close to my life, I'll talk about bass fishing.

I've gone out fishing all day on the boat. If we want to be there just when the fish are biting, from what I'm told, it is at or before dawn (don't quote me on that). Let's say dawn is at six a.m. The lake is about an hour away; say we need to leave at five a.m, maybe four-forty five a.m, just to be safe. It would be best to have the boat completely ready so we can leave exactly when we need to. We'll spend around two or three hours the night before preparing tackle boxes, fishing rods, and the boat itself. All of which will need to be done after work, so we can start at seven and be done by ten p.m. Perfect. Morning comes; we wake up and head out. Need to buy some live worms, obviously. Stop at a gas station, grab a bite to eat (not the worms, that's separate from the bite to eat), top off the gas, get a drink (again, separate from the gasoline, probably a Red Bull), and get the worms. Finally, we've made our way to the lake; now it's time to launch the boat. Done carefully so neither the boat, boat trailer, or truck are damaged. Once afloat, almost right at six a.m, the fishing begins. Hours pass by, and the day gets hotter. More fish don't bite than those that do, but we catch a few, we eat some packed lunches, and around two p.m we decide to call it. Time to get the boat back on the trailer, carefully, of course. Hour drive home. Once home, we've got to undo all the preparations done on the boat. A quicker process, but still about an hour and a half. By this time, it's four-thirty p.m. A solid day of bass fishing!

Can you see the similarities to a regular nine to five job in the above paragraph? Get up early, prepare for work, go to work, eat lunch, come home, and prepare for the day to come. 14 hours were put into this hobby. For some, it sounds like a dream day. For others, it sounds like hell. Regardless, it can't be ignored that it takes just as much, if not more, time and energy to play as it would to have a full day at work. Albeit, bass fisherman would much rather bass fish than work. After a few years, they've got it down to a science and shaved down the preparation time. Much like anybody in any career would, they've found tricks to make the process quicker.

What does this have to do with emotional resilience? Well, part of emotional resilience is finding ways to be as productive as possible. In our hobbies and in our careers, we want to be productive. More productivity results in more profitability, and I'm not strictly talking about money.

My levels of productivity changed when I redefined "play"

for myself. I am not good at relaxing. Never have been. I'm too wired all the time to stop moving, stop thinking, an stop working. I've got to always be doing something. I've always equated play with relaxation. That we participate in hobbies to relax. Over time, I learned that wasn't true. Yet, I hadn't replaced the definition of play. Until now, I presently regard everything I do as work rather than play.

To use this book as an example, some would regard writing it as a hobby. A hobby, by definition, is done in leisure time for pleasure. While I do find great pleasure in writing, it is by no means an activity done leisurely. I currently work from seven a.m to four p.m and spend at least three hours afterwards writing. I consider writing time as my work after work. My five to nine, so to speak. Otherwise, I would get home from work exhausted and spend my time on social media, watching TV, listening to music, or doing other activities that truly require no work. I know myself well enough that going directly home after work would almost always result in the above-mentioned things. Working around this, I go to the gym and then out to my parents house immediately. The passion I find in writing is met with the time I give to write. That time meets the required work the passion needs to thrive.

In this mentality, I am playing whilst I work. But it's work nonetheless! I'd like to add my full support to Mr. Watt's phrase, "...don't imagine for one minute that you've got to be serious about it" (Watts, n.d). There's a balance here as well, but for the most part, we can sense when the time and place merit seriousness. Once a week at church, I'm more serious than any other time. Even then, I ensure to bring an appropriate lightheartedness to keep things interesting for myself. Whether you are playing or working, have fun. Crack jokes to those around you. I grew up teasing my siblings and being teased back. Teasing, when done for the intention of playfulness, adds a gaiety to life's circumstances. Laughter is the best medicine. The best part is, you can't overdose on laughter. You don't need a prescription; it's not a controlled substance. You don't even have to go to the doctor to get a laugh. Laugh a little.

Now, there is a time and a place for relaxation. Sometimes, we need to recuperate and recharge. Or, just decompress. Decompress to help you process. However, we are filled with a capacity for hard work that doesn't require days of recuperation. Capacity levels will vary from person to person, condition to condition. Yet it remains despite different capacities. The trick is to push yourself past that point. Once done, you'll know how much you can take. And you'll learn how much recuperation you need. Please note that the work level capacity will fluctuate. Afterall, we can only confidently rely on change!

Lots of trial and error went into my work level capacity, but once found, I flourished. Eight hours at work, an hour in the gym, and three hours of writing constitute my workday. At the end of the day, around nine-thirty p.m, I wind down. Eat, shower, prepare for bed, read a book for a few minutes, and then I'm in bed around 10:45 p.m. A short time to recharge, yes, but very potent. Very effective.

Without seeing my play as my work, those things I play in would not get done. I'd be left unfulfilled with no goals reached, problems solved, and too much leisure time. Which brings me to the main point of this section. A leisurely life. A life filled with more leisure time than work, though attractive, does not satisfy. Living a life full of leisure leaves you feeling unfulfilled. I truly believe that we do not *need* hours or days to rest from our labors. We have got to be slightly stressed, slightly stimulated, and slightly motivated to feel eventual satisfaction. Work of any degree precedes proper satisfaction. Satisfaction, closely related to happiness, will offer us peace in doing desired deeds. Do not shortchange yourself tomorrow by partaking in illusive leisure today. Acknowledging that our circumstances are drastically different, the best I can do is present my experience, hoping you can take from it small ideas to the betterment of your own life. If I could give you specifics for your life on this matter, I would. But learning the relationship between the leisure level and work level capacity will be far more potent and lasting than merely reading the principle.

Chapter 13
Concluding Thoughts

I'd like to offer a sort of summary of the principles I've now discussed. I will admit that after writing them, I asked myself, "What does this have to do with developing emotional resilience?" for some time, I strained to find an answer. Without relating to emotional resilience, all that I've shared would be pointless. Without intention, we lack progression. I will list each principle and then add commentary explaining how it relates. I've got to make sure this information from my experience is presented clearly so that you may learn from it.

Emotional resilience is a muscle. A muscle needs stress to grow stronger. When we lift weights or exercise, we are purposefully putting stress on our muscles. Once under stress and damaged, our muscles repair themselves. After that repair, they are more capable of withstanding more stress. They can take, lift, and handle more weight. That's how we build strong muscles. As expressed by Nassim Nicholas Taleb, we are antifragile. We grow from stress, chaos, disorder, constant change, and so on. Many of the principles are centered around purposefully creating the contraction necessary for positive growth. Emotional resilience is the product of personal applied contraction to our passions, desires, and natural tendencies.

Emotions Are Cool

The foundation of emotional resilience is an acceptance of emotions. All and every emotion. After acceptance, the choice of management follows. Unlike lifting weights, we don't have to go to the gym to use the weights that will stress our resilience emotionally. Life will always find a way to give you an immense set of emotions to manage. That's cool. Such an opportunity deserves reverence and respect. Open up to all potential opportunities for progress.

Justify the Suffering

Built upon the foundation of emotion, we have in our arsenal the things that give purpose to the pain. It's easier to take one step after another when focussing on what lies ahead, knowing it's valued at a price well worth the cost. Planned, future enjoyment creates present discipline. Some people exercise to *look* a certain way. With an ideal image of how they want to look, they set a course to achieve that. It's a goal. With emotions, we will hold ourselves accountable and shape resilience by accepting pressure (the suffering) as a means to attain pleasure (the justification). Much like the growth of a muscle, consistent stress will lead to a stronger muscle. So it is with our resilience to life's punches. We set milestones, big or small, which, when achieved and worked towards, justify our suffering.

Commit to Fight

With our sights set, we must anchor ourselves to the daily battle of development. Understanding emotions won't leave, we react as we please, and we have things to look forward to. It is now time to *live* the suffering we've justified. With the inevitable ups and downs of life, our emotional muscles grow tough. Able to withstand the more stress put onto us. As the great bodybuilding champion Ronnie Coleman once said, "Everybody wants to be a bodybuilder, but nobody wants to lift no heavy-ass weights" (Coleman, n.d.). Bodybuilders justify the suffering of lifting weights (an ideal look), and then they follow through with actually lifting (committing to the fight).

Enjoy Your Happiness

In my experience, most of my days are spent within the trenches of my own head. Dealing with daily depression exhausts me, yet I am committed to fight. There will be, as there always have been, pockets of happiness that will shine brightly. Though in the middle of the war, we have reserved rights to enjoy the breaks life will offer us. When lifting weights, we can see the progression over time, not only as our physique changes but also in the increase of weight lifted. Moments will be had of admiring the physical change taking place, and in like fashion, we can enjoy times blessed with happiness. Those times are the rest areas as we travel along our road of life. Remember, the primary goal is an inner joy created by our love for life, and happy moments are no more than momentary bonuses on our excursion.

Leave the Money

A large detriment to emotional resilience lies in living in a world saturated with carnal desires for everything material. Giving into these temptations will only lead to atrophy of the strongest, most important muscle. The potential for great atrophy shows the same great potential for strength. Leaving the money behind forces us to focus outside of ourselves, and onto relationships. We focus on the spiritual, mental, emotional, and physical growth afforded us. Having removed the distraction of money, we now see what lies behind all temporary endeavors - those things which hold the greatest value. Unless removed, we will continue blinded by what promises better vision.

68 Hot, 68 Cold

Life has a particular duality that proves difficult to define. The yin yang works wonders in this regard as we have chaos and order embedded within one another, existing in close quarters. One and the same, yet dramatically different. In regard to emotional resilience, we must acknowledge the chaos of our lives and highlight the order that can be made from it. 68 hot, 68 cold works to show that every challenge also presents an opportunity. Every opportunity presents a challenge. Each moment exists as one entity and as two variations of itself simultaneously. Our feelings will exist no matter what. We must accept their temperature and then control the smolder within if we want to become the most productive. We set the thermostat; we did not create it, however, and must accept its existence. To continue the weight lifting analogy, the weights won't be lighter because we want them to be. The weights can build muscle or destroy them depending on our form. We wield the power of potential.

Outside Auditors

In weight lifting, they say to always use a spotter. The role of a spotter is not to interfere with the actual lifting of the weights. Their responsibility lies in the *safety* of the weightlifter and those around him. Not having a spotter for lifts like the bench press can be very dangerous for the lifter. Unable to push the weight back into the starting position and safely into the rack, the weight can slowly crush the lifter's sternum and throat area. Depending on how heavy the weight is, the activated muscles can strain to injury. A spotter will recognize when help is needed and jump in to assist in the lifting of the bar. At times, the lifter can signal to the spotter that they need help, and in jumps the spotter. In both cases, the spotter cannot lift the entire weight of the bar. So, added strength from the spotter allows for the safe return of the bar and does not shortchange the lifter's exercise. Much like spotters in weightlifting, we ask for help from our outside auditors. They can't lift the burden entirely, but with their assistance, struggles are made somewhat easier. All the while, the emotional resilience muscle benefits from bearing the present burdens. As it would be foolish for a struggling weightlifter not to call on the spotter, the same goes for us who don't ask for help when we need it. More often than not, people around us won't see the inner turmoil we are braving. For this reason, we need a close, tight circle with whom we are willing to vulnerably ask for help. Asking for help shows strength and a desire to better oneself. Suffering in silence is a sign of weakness. You are strong; you are capable. Ask for help.

Leave a Leisure Life

Ralph Parlette said, "The pursuit of easy things makes men weak. Do not equip yourselves with superior power and hope to escape the responsibility and work. It cannot be done. It is following the path of least resistance that makes rivers and men" (Parlette, n.d.). We work with the "superior power" within us to master discipline. Strap on your boots, buckle your seatbelts, and get ready for the work that's ahead. By seeing the work that all things require, we learn the value of working on ourselves and our emotional state. If we can go to work to get paid and then use the money to work on how we play, then we can work to better ourselves for our sake. The payment of such work far exceeds the value of any salary. Much like the brief, happy moments, we will have occasion to lay leisurely. Yet unless bridled, such moments will internally derail our divine progression.

Each of these principles is about the contraction of desires. Contracted to the point of positive stress, which results in stronger emotional muscle and capability. Once again, only you can determine when, in what manner, and for how long this contraction will take place. And only you can choose to benefit. Along with this contraction, each principle deals with reframing definitions of emotion, work, play, suffering, fighting, commitment, and so forth. Learning the principle will facilitate in redefining certain topics in your life. Such reframing, contraction, and redefining are the ingredients for building the emotional resilience foundation. Compounded over time, these ingredients become ingrained in us. Those same ingredients will eventually maintain themselves as we maintain consistency of practice.

SECTION 3

Chapter 14
Why Develop Emotional Resilience?

Much of the motivation to strengthen this muscle was evident as I made that list of many of life's inconveniences. With no shortage of struggle, we need to supply ourselves with an even greater increase of ability to work through that struggle. Reading through those afflictions may not have been enough to convince you of the necessity of emotional resilience. If that is the case, my goal in this section is to further expound on the benefits, as well as the necessity.

I'm pulling all the stops on this section. Quotes, analogies, and probably some made-up words. All intended to get my point across. I am very passionate about this subject, particularly the reasons *why* we must develop this sense. Partly because every day of my life, I see examples in favor of this emotional skill. And if repetition really is the father of learning, then I suggest we take to heart the lessons shown to us every day.

The development of emotional resilience will *not* stop hardships in life. Remember, just because you want the weights in the gym to be lighter, does not make them lighter. Because you are better prepared for life, however, you will have become emotionally mature. Meaning you feel all positive emotions deeper, and, yes, negative emotions as well. To fully experience all that life has to offer, you must do just that. Life has pain. Life has pleasure. If you know pain, then you know pleasure. Desiring happiness breeds fear of sadness. For many years, I could not bear the burdens of negative feelings. Choosing to numb out numbed joy and muffled happy moments as well. I learned if I really strove for joy, I must be prepared to witness tragedy. Be that as it may, infrequent happiness was, and is still, worth it.

All primary desires, for most people, revolve around joy. We do things because we want to have joy. We all want joy, yet we seldom understand the cost associated with this desire. Nothing is free, and that certainly includes inner joy. You see, we only understand joy because we've felt sorrow. The high from happy times only is appreciated after traversing the depth of sorrow. They juxtapose one another. Those days filled with great joy shine brighter in days filled with great sorrow, and vice versa. Two situations will arise as we strive for joy and for happiness. One: Happiness will start to feel farther and farther out of reach. Two: We will begin to recognize struggles in a different light.

The striving causes us to live in the past, desperate for

those happy times to repeat themselves. We do this because, in hard times, we do whatever we can to feel better. The "narcotic of nostalgia" (Neal A. Maxwell) is cathartic. However, living in the past removes us from the present, leaving us empty because emotions are only experienced in the present and learned from in the past. Left with an aching desire we can't attain, we partake of self-pity. Self-pity produces frustration, depression, and unhappiness. Missing out on moments from which happiness could be taken, life seems void of anything worth living for. The same is true for seeking happiness in the future. Phrases like, "I'll be happy when *x,y, or z* take place" or "*If* this happens, *then* I will be happy" discredit present moments in an effort to highlight what we think will be a better time. Unfortunately, the future will *never* be the present. We will *never* experience the future like we do the present. The constant juxtaposition of past happy times and happy times to come constitutes the reason we need to live in the moment. Whether obsessing over the past or anxiously awaiting the future, we paint the present a dismal gray. Just out of reach, we can't feel joy. Because current times do not match what once was or what we expect of them, life becomes nothing but a struggle.

Emotional resilience creates the surface upon which all present moments roll off with little friction. Emotional resilience forces us to remain in the present. Existing in the present gives us the chance to change our circumstances to reach a state we feel most comfortable in. We can only change our immediate circumstances, and they are only apparent in the present. When done properly, we shape both the past and the future by making the most of the present. Hard times and negative emotions will be felt deeper, but if not given the power to overtake us, we will bounce back quicker. Good times and positive emotions will be felt deeper and given the power to lift us higher and longer. We are in sort of a limbo state with emotional resilience, a flow state. Circumstances arise, we respond, we grow, we feel, we love, we cry, we move forward. Finding peace in positivity and growing from negativity. Otherwise, we are unprepared to appreciate life's many gifts. And, as C.S Lewis says, we are "...running about with fire extinguishers when there is a flood.." (Lewis, n.d.).

Emotional resilience proffers us the most out of life. It is the sorbent that takes the most out of all of life's successes and trials. We go about life with an overall *nonchalant* sense. Yet, adopting a nonchalant feeling does not exempt us from the necessary work required to maintain a care-free lifestyle, hence why I've paired these two words together: nonchalant perfectionism.

I acknowledge the danger in suggesting that we don't need to overly concern ourselves with the future or that the past bears no weight on the present. Clearly, without the past, we have nothing from which to learn. Goals (the future) are what we work towards, as they give us a serene feeling of improvement. There is a difference between setting goals for improvement and desperately living in the future. I am suggesting we adopt a *nonchalant* thought process, as well as a *perfectionist* work ethic. Emotional resilience will bridge the gap between these two opposing ideas. Without that gap bridged, we are too lazy. Too comfortable, too complacent. Oversaturated with illusioned joy and life-sucking leisure. Or, we are too uptight. Too wound up, too stressed. Too unhappy with our mediocre performances compared to unrealistic ideals of our performance. Thus, I left yearning for a small sip of earned joy. There must exist within us a mediator which governs our highs and our lows. To experience life to its fullest is why we develop emotional resilience.

Stronger emotional resilience allows us to run *through* the storms faster. Heck, it gives us the ability to *want* to run through the storm as opposed to *from* it. No longer are we under the control of our inner demons dead set on our destruction. No longer do we allow for upsets to dictate our day. "..did you have a bad day or a bad five minutes that you milked all day?" I don't know who said that, and I don't know where I heard it either. It fits well, though. No longer will a bad five minutes constitute the next 24 hours. Expanded further, we won't let a bad hour dictate our day. An honest bad day won't dictate the week! Neither the month to the year nor the year to the decade! No. We are *resilient*. We move forward, appreciating the past's lessons, appropriately focusing on future goals, and loving the present moment.

Joy is the product of work. Although work typically sucks, we can't get away from it. Any worthwhile venture requires work. Whether physical, mental, emotional, intellectual, or spiritual, there are things to do. Tasks to complete. Always we work. When approached head-on, that work will result in increased self-worth and joy. Satisfaction follows work. In part, because once finished, we no longer have to work for a time! Trust me, when I clock out of my job to finish the workday, I've got a 'Snickers Satisfies' smile on my face. It feels *happy* to complete tasks. Even more so when our efforts are expended on creating. Or expansion on connection with ourselves or others. Emotional resilience acknowledges necessary work, attacks it, completes it, and integrates the affixed satisfaction within us. All while deflecting frustrations from our pointed productivity.

When climbing uphill and completing tasks, emotional resilience keeps us moving. It is no easy feat moving forward amidst overwhelming adversity. And so we must have developed the muscle which takes those steps. Greater inner rewards follow greater exertions of growth. Developing this skill broadens the perspective that appreciates the journey. This is not the cliche, "joy is in the journey," because truthfully, the journey sucks sometimes. I find I am more often trudging than I am journeying. So I can appreciate the journey rather than fall in love with it. Some journeys just suck. But it is our perspective that keeps us going. Emotional resilience turns our Mount Everests into "pale blue dot(s)" (Segan & Druyan, 2011).

We really must only keep going. Boiled down to the simplest form, that's all we can do. We cannot stop. We must endure; we must go on. I've tried to take the path that leads to a dead stop. And I can tell you there is no light at the bottom of that barrel. I can also tell you that surrounded by darkness, you can produce your own inner light, which will hold you strong till the darkness disperses. And if but only for a small moment does the light remain, it will burn bright enough to fuel each step back into and through the darkness.

I'd like to end where I more or less began - with you. You are the catalyst. The benefactor and the benefitted. The protagonist. And, at times, the antagonist. The decision maker of your destiny. You are *it*. If for nothing else, develop this skill for yourself. We must care about ourselves as much as we care for others. As Jordan Peterson said, "Treat yourself like someone you are responsible for helping." It is not selfish to better develop yourself. In doing so, you will increase your capacity to help those around you. Those you associate with cannot develop this skill on your behalf. You must act. You must stand up, rise up, and look up. You must activate the lion within that pushes your ambitions toward fruition.

We are, unfortunately, alone within our own minds. The plight of all people revolves around clearly conveying their deepest desire by means of self-expression. Develop this skill to better understand yourself and how to tolerate (for better or for worse) those who fumble in their attempt at self-expression. The cry of every human heart is to feel loved. It is to feel heard. Far too often, we are under-loved and under-heard. We must buoy ourselves to stay above neglect, unintentional or otherwise.

No matter how much we love others, they will let us down. Our parents, siblings, children, cousins, uncles, aunts, grandparents, close friends, acquaintances, coworkers, bosses, neighbors, community leaders, church leaders, politicians, celebrities, musicians, artists, writers, and everyone else will at some point fail to meet your expectations. Regardless of the love you have for them, they will come up short. Not always, but often. It will happen. You cannot expect to place responsibility for your joy in the hands of people who already have too much to handle. You will be let down far more often than you already are. I, for one, don't want to add more disappointments from others to my life. If we can help it, which we can, letdowns will be nothing more than insignificant inconveniences.

Some people *want* to harm others emotionally and physically. Those people deserve every damnation available. For the most part, I believe people don't seek to inflict harm on others. And so, when lapses in kindness arise, you must recognize that it's not all about you. We all are walking this boulevard alone at different speeds. The boulevard has traffic, and with traffic comes accidents, at your fault on occasion and at the fault of others at times. The responsive actions that follow are formative in who you are. Will you show respect and likewise earn it?

Race, sexual orientation, gender, or any other label do not exempt us from personal, inner, and emotional responsibility of ourselves, and ourselves only. You cannot force your beliefs, ideas, pronouns, desires, religion, or thoughts on someone else and be surprised when you feel resistance. Relationships, romantic or otherwise, are the confluence of people who see beauty in the humanity of the other person. Setting aside expectations, we come together in expressions of love, friendship, and charity. The construction of relationships is the product of connecting with other people. Connecting is the cure. With yourself and with others. Take away connecting, and you take away the very thing that gives us life. We need emotional resilience to make it through our life.

Life's curriculum is too volatile to allow room for emotional fragility.

References

Books

Danforth, W. H. (2006). *I dare you!*. Cosimo, Inc..

Goggins, D. (2021). *Can't Hurt Me: Master Your Mind and Defy the Odds*. David Goggins.

Sagan, C., & Druyan, A. (2011). *Pale blue dot: A vision of the human future in space*. Ballantine books.

Tzu, S. (2005). *The art of war: Complete texts and commentaries*. Shambhala Publications.

Willink, J., & Babin, L. (2017). *Extreme ownership: How US Navy SEALs lead and win*. St. Martin's Press.

Speeches

Monson, T. S. (2021, March 15). *Decisions determine destiny.* BYU Speeches. https://speeches.byu.edu/talks/thomas-s-monson/decisions-determine-destiny/

Watts, A. (n.d.). *Work and play.* The Library. https://www. organism.earth/library/document/essential-lectures-7

Songs

BlackAlicious (Ft. Gil Scott-Heron) – first in flight. (n.d.). Genius. https://genius.com/Blackalicious-first-in-flight-lyrics

Daniel Johnston says in his song "Don't Let the Sun go Go Down on Your Grievances," - Bing. (n.d.). Bing. https://www.bing.com/search?q=Daniel+Johnston+-says+in+his+song+%E2%80%9CDon%E2%80%99t+Let+the+Sun+go+Go+Down+on+Your+Grievances%2C%E2%80%9D&cvid=a47852ed086b4ba6a1e74ef6ed-cd8206&gs_lcrp=EgZjaHJvbWUyBggAEEUYODIBBzczM-mowajmoAgCwAgA&FORM=ANAB01&PC=EDGEDBB

Kendrick Lamar (Ft. Anna Wise, Bilal & Snoop Dogg) – Institutionalized. (n.d.). Genius. https://genius.com/Kendrick-lamar-institutionalized-lyrics

Larry Fisherman (Ft. Mac Miller) – Smile. (n.d.). Genius. https://genius.com/Larry-fisherman-smile-lyrics

Slife. (2021, July 13). *Serenity prayer.* The Spiritual Life. https://slife.org/serenity-prayer/#:~:text=Reinhold%20Niebuhr%27s%20The%20Serenity%20Prayer%3A%20Living%20one%20day,time%2C%20Accepting%20hardship%20as%20the%20pathway%20to%20peace.

The visible surface of the sun appears to be in full boil, by I win I lose. (2019, October 22). I Win I Lose. https://iwinilose. bandcamp.com/track/the-visible-surface-of-the-sun-appears-to-be-in-full-boil

Tyler, The Creator – Enjoy Right Now, Today. (n.d.). Genius. https://genius.com/Tyler-the-creator-enjoy-right-now-today-lyrics

Biblical Sources

Matthew 6:24 (NIV). (n.d.). Bible Gateway. https://www. biblegateway.com/passage/?search=Matthew%20 6:24&version=NIV

Luke 9:24 (KJV). (n.d.). Bible Gateway. https://www. biblegateway.com/passage/?search=Luke%20 9:24&version=KJV#:~:text=Luke%209%3A24%20King%20 James%20Version%2024%20For%20whosoever,for%20 my%20sake%2C%20the%20same%20shall%20save%20it.

1 *Corinthians 12:2 - Bible Gateway.* (n.d.). https://www. biblegateway.com/verse/en/1%20Corinthians%2012%3A2

Proverbs 16:18 - The Reply of the Tongue is from the LORD. (n.d.). Bible Hub. https://biblehub.com/proverbs/16-18.htm

Movies

Holes movie Review. (2003, September 22). Common Sense Media. https://www.commonsensemedia.org/movie-reviews/holes

Into the Wild (2007) | Adventure, biography, drama. (2007, October 19). IMDb. https://www.imdb.com/title/tt0758758/

PowerfulJRE. (2018, November 30). *Joe Rogan Experience #1208 - Jordan Peterson* [Video]. YouTube. https://www.youtube.com/watch?v=vIeFt88Hm8s

Poems

A Servant To Servants, by Robert Frost. (n.d.). https://www.robertfrost.org/a-servant-to-servants.jsp

Quotes

A quote by Ralph Parlette. (n.d.). https://www.goodreads.com/quotes/42464-strength-and-struggle-go-together-the-supreme-reward-of-struggle#:~:text=%E2%80%9CStrength%20and%20struggle%20go%20together.%20The%20supreme%20reward,and%20hope%20to%20escape%20the%20responsibility%20and%20work.

A quote by Ronnie Coleman. (n.d.). https://www.goodreads.com/quotes/526415-everybody-wants-to-be-a-bodybuilder-but-nobody-wants-to

A quote from The Screwtape Letters. (n.d.). https://www.goodreads.com/quotes/79751-the-game-is-to-have-them-all-running-about-with#:~:text=C.S.%20Lewis%20%3E%20Quotes%20%3E%20Quotable%20Quote%20%28%3F%29,gunwale%20under.%E2%80%9D%20%E2%80%95%20C.S.%20Lewis%2C%20The%20Screwtape%20Letters

Barry. (2013, June 2). "You're more likely to act yourself into feeling than feel yourself into action." - The Quotable Coach

%. The Quotable Coach. https://www.thequotablecoach.
com/youre-more-likely-to-act-yourself-into-feeling-than-
feel-yourself-into-action/

Holmes, M. (2011, June 25). "It's not about the money. It's about
sending a message!" WhatCulture.com. https://whatculture.
com/film/its-not-about-the-money-its-about-sending-a-
message

https://blogdigger.com/a-person-who-thinks-all-the-
time/#:~:text=Alan%20Watts%2C%20a%20British%20
philosopher%2C%20said%20that%20a,not%20aware%20
of%20what%20is%20happening%20around%20him.

Ralph Parlette Quotes (Author of The University of Hard Knocks).
(n.d.). https://www.goodreads.com/author/quotes/809509.
Ralph_Parlette#:~:text=The%20pursuit%20of%20easy%20
things%20makes%20men%20weak.,least%20resistance%20
that%20makes%20rivers%20and%20men%20crooked.

Vargas, I. (2018, July 10). "How You Do Anything is How You
Do Everything" — V1H CONSULTING. V1H CONSULTING.
https://v1hconsulting.com/articles/2018/7/10/how-you-
do-anything-is-how-you-do-everything

Martha Beck quotes. (n.d.). BrainyQuote. https://www.
brainyquote.com/quotes/martha_beck_655244

Holmes, M. (2011b, June 25). "It's not about the money. It's about
sending a message!" WhatCulture.com. https://whatculture.
com/film/its-not-about-the-money-its-about-sending-a-
message

Printed in Great Britain
by Amazon

40852529R00098